THE
FAMILY RECORD

Published by Town House, 42 Morehampton Road, Donnybrook, Dublin 4, Ireland
Copyright © Thomas P. Cleary. 1st edition 1977, 2nd edition 1988, reprinted 1993.

ISBN: 0-948524-13-8

Printed in Ireland by Criterion Press, Dublin

THE FAMILY RECORD has been devised to facilitate the compilation of genealogical data, in simple but comprehensive form, going back over five generations and going forward three. This span has been selected as coming within the average scope of living knowledge or within easy recall without tedious research.

The album is designed to allow an almost limitless extension of information should the compiler(s) wish to do so. Extra pages are provided at regular intervals. While specific pages have been allocated for first cousins, blank pages are given to accommodate second and third cousins. Self-adhesive stickers may be used to substitute titles or subtitles, if required.

A simple system of colour-coding clearly identifies the male and female compiler's sections: blue for the male, green for the female.

The publishers would strongly advise that details be entered in pencil at first, so that corrections may be made without difficulty.

Gradual expansion and development of the work should provide a fascinating and revealing study with an ultimate and permanent dossier of antecedents, as well as a useful and ready-to-hand documentation for biographical reference. This compilation does not pretend to be in itself a complete genealogical study but it may inspire further research and elaboration through information gleaned from parish registers, wills, census records, heritage centres and libraries.

(The Family Record is dedicated to my mother, Anastatia — T.P.C.)

CONTENTS

(Devised by Thomas P. Cleary)

FAMILY RECORD

of

. . . .

of

. . . .

. . . .

. . . .

This record was begun on the . . . . .day of. . . . . .in the year. . . . .

Signature . . . .

To be filled in by either male or female single compiler.

FAMILY RECORD

of   and

....

of

....

who were married in

....

....

on the .... day of .... in the year........

The ceremony was performed by

....

in the presence of witnesses

....

and

....

This record was begun on the ....day of..........in the year..........

Signatures...

....

MALE COMPILER'S CHART

GREAT GREAT GRANDPARENTS	GREAT GRANDPARENTS	GRAND PARENTS	FATHER
. . . .			
. . . .			
	. . . .		
	. . . .		
. . . .		. . . .	
. . . .		. . . .	
. . . .			
. . . .	. . . .		
	. . . .		
. . . .			. . . .
. . . .			
. . . .			. . . .
. . . .	. . . .		
	. . . .		
. . . .		. . . .	
. . . .			M.
		. . . .	
. . . .			
. . . .	. . . .		. . . .
	. . . .		
. . . .			. . . .

MALE COMPILER'S CHART

MOTHER	GRAND PARENTS	GREAT GRANDPARENTS	GREAT GREAT GRANDPARENTS
			. . . .
			. . . .
		. . . .	. . . .
		. . . .	
			. . . .
	. . . .		. . . .
	. . . .		. . . .
		. . . .	. . . .
		. . . .	
			. . . .
. . . .			
			. . . .
. . . .			. . . .
		. . . .	
		. . . .	. . . .
			. . . .
	. . . .		
MPILER			. . . .
	. . . .		
			. . . .
. . . .		. . . .	. . . .
		. . . .	
. . . .			. . . .
			. . . .

9

BRIEF BIOGRAPHY

Surname ....

Given Name(s) ....

Nationality ....

Date of Birth ....

Place of Birth ....

....

Marital Status ....

Religion ....

Occupation ....

....

Height/Weight ....

Colour of Hair/Eyes ....

Schools ....

....

....

Achievements ....

....

....

....

Additional Information

....

....

....

....

....

....

....

....

....

....

....

....

....

....

....

....

....

....

PATERNAL LINE

FATHER

Surname	....
Given Name(s)	....
	....
Nationality	....
Date of Birth	....
Place of Birth	....
	....
Home Address(es)	....
	....
	....
	....
Occupation	....
	....
Religion	....
Date of Marriage(s)	....
	....
Date of Death	....
Place of Burial	....

Additional Information

....

....

....

....

....

....

....

....

....

....

....

....

....

....

....

....

PATERNAL LINE

FATHER'S BROTHERS (UNCLES)

Surname	....	....	....
Given Name(s)	....	....	....
	....	....	....
Nationality	....	....	....
Date of Birth	....	....	....
Place of Birth	....	....	....
	....	....	....
Home Address(es)	....	....	....
	....	....	....
	....	....	....
	....	....	....
Occupation	....	....	....
	....	....	....
Religion	....	....	....
Date of Marriage(s)	....	....	....
	....	....	....
	....	....	....
Date of Death	....	....	....
Place of Burial	....	....	....

FATHER'S BROTHERS (UNCLES)

Surname	....	....	....
Given Name(s)	....	....	....
	....	....	....
Nationality	....	....	....
Date of Birth	....	....	....
Place of Birth	....	....	....
	....	....	....
Home Address(es)	....	....	....
	....	....	....
	....	....	....
	....	....	....
Occupation	....	....	....
	....	....	....
Religion	....	....	....
Date of Marriage(s)	....	....	....
	....	....	....
	....	....	....
Date of Death	....	....	....
Place of Burial	....	....	....

PATERNAL LINE

FATHER'S BROTHERS' CHILDREN (FIRST COUSINS)

Surname . . . .

Given Name(s) . . . .

Surname . . . .

Given Name(s) . . . .

Surname . . . .

Given Name(s) . . . .

Surname . . . .

Given Name(s) . . . .

Surname . . . .

Given Name(s) . . . .

Surname . . . .

Given Name(s) . . . .

Surname . . . .

Given Name(s) . . . .

Child of . . . .

and . . . .

Child of . . . .

and . . . .

Child of . . . .

and . . . .

Child of . . . .

and . . . .

Child of . . . .

and . . . .

Child of . . . .

and . . . .

Child of . . . .

and . . . .

PATERNAL LINE

FATHER'S BROTHERS' CHILDREN (FIRST COUSINS)

Surname .... Child of ....

Given Name(s) .... and ....

Surname .... Child of ....

Given Name(s) .... and ....

Surname .... Child of ....

Given Name(s) .... and ....

Surname .... Child of ....

Given Name(s) .... and ....

Surname .... Child of ....

Given Name(s) .... and ....

Surname .... Child of ....

Given Name(s) .... and ....

Surname .... Child of ....

Given Name(s) .... and ....

Surname .... Child of ....

Given Name(s) .... and ....

Surname .... Child of ....

Given Name(s) .... and ....

FATHER'S SISTERS (AUNTS)

Surname	....	....	....
Given Name(s)	....	....	....
	....	....	....
Nationality	....	....	....
Date of Birth	....	....	....
Place of Birth	....	....	....
	....	....	....
Home Address(es)	....	....	....
	....	....	....
	....	....	....
	....	....	....
Occupation	....	....	....
Religion	....	....	....
Date of Marriage(s)	....	....	....
	....	....	....
	....	....	....
Married Name	....	....	....
Date of Death	....	....	....
Place of Burial	....	....	....

FATHER'S SISTERS (AUNTS)

Surname	....	....	....
Given Name(s)	....	....	....
	....	....	....
Nationality	....	....	....
Date of Birth	....	....	....
Place of Birth	....	....	....
	....	....	....
Home Address(es)	....	....	....
	....	....	....
	....	....	....
	....	....	....
Occupation	....	....	....
Religion	....	....	....
Date of Marriage(s)	....	....	....
	....	....	....
	....	....	....
Married Name	....	....	....
Date of Death	....	....	....
Place of Burial	....	....	....

PATERNAL LINE

FATHER'S SISTERS' CHILDREN (FIRST COUSINS)

Surname ....   Child of ....

Given Name(s) ....   and ....

Surname ....   Child of ....

Given Name(s) ....   and ....

Surname ....   Child of ....

Given Name(s) ....   and ....

Surname ....   Child of ....

Given Name(s) ....   and ....

Surname ....   Child of ....

Given Name(s) ....   and ....

Surname ....   Child of ....

Given Name(s) ....   and ....

Surname ....   Child of ....

Given Name(s) ....   and ....

Surname ....   Child of ....

Given Name(s) ....   and ....

Surname ....   Child of ....

Given Name(s) ....   and ....

PATERNAL LINE

FATHER'S SISTERS' CHILDREN (FIRST COUSINS)

Surname . . . .   Child of . . . .

Given Name(s) . . . .   and . . . .

Surname . . . .   Child of . . . .

Given Name(s) . . . .   and . . . .

Surname . . . .   Child of . . . .

Given Name(s) . . . .   and . . . .

Surname . . . .   Child of . . . .

Given Name(s) . . . .   and . . . .

Surname . . . .   Child of . . . .

Given Name(s) . . . .   and . . . .

Surname . . . .   Child of . . . .

Given Name(s) . . . .   and . . . .

Surname . . . .   Child of . . . .

Given Name(s) . . . .   and . . . .

Surname . . . .   Child of . . . .

Given Name(s) . . . .   and . . . .

ADDITIONAL INFORMATION

PATERNAL LINE

GRANDFATHER (FATHER'S FATHER)

Surname	. . . . Additional Information
Given Name(s)	. . . .
	. . . .
Nationality	. . . .
Date of Birth	. . . .
Place of Birth	. . . .
	. . . .
Home Address(es)	. . . .
	. . . .
	. . . .
	. . . .
Occupation	. . . .
	. . . .
Religion	. . . .
Date of Marriage(s)	. . . .
	. . . .
	. . . .
Date of Death	. . . .
Place of Burial	. . . .

GRANDFATHER'S BROTHERS (GREAT-UNCLES)

Surname	....	....	....
Given Name(s)	....	....	....
	....	....	....
Nationality	....	....	....
Date of Birth	....	....	....
Place of Birth	....	....	....
	....	....	....
Home Address(es)	....	....	....
	....	....	....
	....	....	....
	....	....	....
Occupation	....	....	....
	....	....	....
Religion	....	....	....
Date of Marriage(s)	....	....	....
	....	....	....
	....	....	....
Date of Death	....	....	....
Place of Burial	....	....	....

GRANDFATHER'S BROTHERS (GREAT-UNCLES)

Surname	....	....	....
Given Name(s)	....	....	....
	....	....	....
Nationality	....	....	....
Date of Birth	....	....	....
Place of Birth	....	....	....
	....	....	....
Home Address(es)	....	....	....
	....	....	....
	....	....	....
	....	....	....
Occupation	....	....	....
	....	....	....
Religion	....	....	....
Date of Marriage(s)	....	....	....
	....	....	....
	....	....	....
Date of Death	....	....	....
Place of Burial	....	....	....

GRANDFATHER'S BROTHERS' CHILDREN (FIRST COUSINS ONCE REMOVED)

Surname	....	Child of	....
Given Name(s)	....	and	....
Surname	....	Child of	....
Given Name(s)	....	and	....
Surname	....	Child of	....
Given Name(s)	....	and	....
Surname	....	Child of	....
Given Name(s)	....	and	....
Surname	....	Child of	....
Given Name(s)	....	and	....
Surname	....	Child of	....
Given Name(s)	....	and	....
Surname	....	Child of	....
Given Name(s)	....	and	....
Surname	....	Child of	....
Given Name(s)	....	and	....

GRANDFATHER'S SISTERS (GREAT-AUNTS)

Surname	. . . .	. . . .	. . . .
Given Name(s)	. . . .	. . . .	. . . .
	. . . .	. . . .	. . . .
Nationality	. . . .	. . . .	. . . .
Date of Birth	. . . .	. . . .	. . . .
Place of Birth	. . . .	. . . .	. . . .
	. . . .	. . . .	. . . .
Home Address(es)	. . . .	. . . .	. . . .
	. . . .	. . . .	. . . .
	. . . .	. . . .	. . . .
	. . . .	. . . .	. . . .
Occupation	. . . .	. . . .	. . . .
	. . . .	. . . .	. . . .
Religion	. . . .	. . . .	. . . .
Date of Marriage(s)	. . . .	. . . .	. . . .
	. . . .	. . . .	. . . .
Married Name	. . . .	. . . .	. . . .
Date of Death	. . . .	. . . .	. . . .
Place of Burial	. . . .	. . . .	. . . .

GRANDFATHER'S SISTERS (GREAT-AUNTS)

Surname	....	....	....
Given Name(s)	....	....	....
	....	....	....
Nationality	....	....	....
Date of Birth	....	....	....
Place of Birth	....	....	....
	....	....	....
Home Address(es)	....	....	....
	....	....	....
	....	....	....
	....	....	....
Occupation	....	....	....
	....	....	....
Religion	....	....	....
Date of Marriage(s)	....	....	....
	....	....	....
Married Name	....	....	....
Date of Death	....	....	....
Place of Burial	....	....	....

GRANDFATHER'S SISTERS' CHILDREN (FIRST COUSINS ONCE REMOVED)

Surname	....	Child of	....
Given Name(s)	....	and	....
Surname	....	Child of	....
Given Name(s)	....	and	....
Surname	....	Child of	....
Given Name(s)	....	and	....
Surname	....	Child of	....
Given Name(s)	....	and	....
Surname	....	Child of	....
Given Name(s)	....	and	....
Surname	....	Child of	....
Given Name(s)	....	and	....
Surname	....	Child of	....
Given Name(s)	....	and	....
Surname	....	Child of	....
Given Name(s)	....	and	....

GRANDMOTHER (FATHER'S MOTHER)

Surname .... Additional Information

Given Name(s) ....

....

Nationality ....

Date of Birth ....

Place of Birth ....

....

Home Address(es) ....

....

....

....

Occupation ....

....

Religion ....

Date of Marriage(s) ....

....

Married Name ....

Date of Death ....

Place of Burial ....

PATERNAL LINE

GRANDMOTHER'S BROTHERS (GREAT-UNCLES)

Surname	. . . .	. . . .	. . . .
Given Name(s)	. . . .	. . . .	. . . .
	. . . .	. . . .	. . . .
Nationality	. . . .	. . . .	. . . .
Date of Birth	. . . .	. . . .	. . . .
Place of Birth	. . . .	. . . .	. . . .
	. . . .	. . . .	. . . .
Home Address(es)	. . . .	. . . .	. . . .
	. . . .	. . . .	. . . .
	. . . .	. . . .	. . . .
	. . . .	. . . .	. . . .
Occupation	. . . .	. . . .	. . . .
	. . . .	. . . .	. . . .
Religion	. . . .	. . . .	. . . .
Date of Marriage(s)	. . . .	. . . .	. . . .
	. . . .	. . . .	. . . .
	. . . .	. . . .	. . . .
Date of Death	. . . .	. . . .	. . . .
Place of Burial	. . . .	. . . .	. . . .

GRANDMOTHER'S BROTHERS (GREAT-UNCLES)

Surname	....	....	....
Given Name(s)	....	....	....
	....	....	....
Nationality	....	....	....
Date of Birth	....	....	....
Place of Birth	....	....	....
	....	....	....
Home Address(es)	....	....	....
	....	....	....
	....	....	....
	....	....	....
Occupation	....	....	....
	....	....	....
Religion	....	....	....
Date of Marriage(s)	....	....	....
	....	....	....
	....	....	....
Date of Death	....	....	....
Place of Burial	....	....	....

GRANDMOTHER'S BROTHERS' CHILDREN (FIRST COUSINS ONCE REMOVED)

Surname .... Child of ....

Given Name(s) .... and ....

Surname .... Child of ....

Given Name(s) .... and ....

Surname .... Child of ....

Given Name(s) .... and ....

Surname .... Child of ....

Given Name(s) .... and ....

Surname .... Child of ....

Given Name(s) .... and ....

Surname .... Child of ....

Given Name(s) .... and ....

Surname .... Child of ....

Given Name(s) .... and ....

Surname .... Child of ....

Given Name(s) .... and ....

Surname .... Child of ....

Given Name(s) .... and ....

GRANDMOTHER'S SISTERS (GREAT-AUNTS)

Surname			
Given Name(s)			
Nationality			
Date of Birth			
Place of Birth			
Home Address(es)			
Occupation			
Religion			
Date of Marriage(s)			
Married Name			
Date of Death			
Place of Burial			

GRANDMOTHER'S SISTERS (GREAT-AUNTS)

Surname	. . . .	. . . .	. . . .
Given Name(s)	. . . .	. . . .	. . . .
	. . . .	. . . .	. . . .
Nationality	. . . .	. . . .	. . . .
Date of Birth	. . . .	. . . .	. . . .
Place of Birth	. . . .	. . . .	. . . .
	. . . .	. . . .	. . . .
Home Address(es)	. . . .	. . . .	. . . .
	. . . .	. . . .	. . . .
	. . . .	. . . .	. . . .
	. . . .	. . . .	. . . .
Occupation	. . . .	. . . .	. . . .
	. . . .	. . . .	. . . .
Religion	. . . .	. . . .	. . . .
Date of Marriage(s)	. . . .	. . . .	. . . .
	. . . .	. . . .	. . . .
Married Name	. . . .	. . . .	. . . .
Date of Death	. . . .	. . . .	. . . .
Place of Burial	. . . .	. . . .	. . . .

GRANDMOTHER'S SISTERS' CHILDREN (FIRST COUSINS ONCE REMOVED)

Surname	....	Child of	....
Given Name(s)	....	and	....
Surname	....	Child of	....
Given Name(s)	....	and	....
Surname	....	Child of	....
Given Name(s)	....	and	....
Surname	....	Child of	....
Given Name(s)	....	and	....
Surname	....	Child of	....
Given Name(s)	....	and	....
Surname	....	Child of	....
Given Name(s)	....	and	....
Surname	....	Child of	....
Given Name(s)	....	and	....
Surname	....	Child of	....
Given Name(s)	....	and	....

....

....

....

....

....

....

....

....

....

....

....

....

....

....

....

....

....

....

....

....

....

....

....

....

....

....

....

....

....

....

....

....

GREAT-GRANDFATHER (FATHER'S FATHER'S FATHER)

Surname ....   Additional Information

Given Name(s) ....

....

Nationality ....

Date of Birth ....

Place of Birth ....

....

Home Address(es) ....

....

....

....

Occupation ....

....

Religion ....

Date of Marriage(s) ....

....

....

Date of Death ....

Place of Burial ....

GREAT-GRANDFATHER'S BROTHERS (GREAT-GREAT-UNCLES)

Surname	....	....	....
Given Name(s)	....	....	....
	....	....	....
Nationality	....	....	....
Date of Birth	....	....	....
Place of Birth	....	....	....
	....	....	....
Home Address(es)	....	....	....
	....	....	....
	....	....	....
	....	....	....
Occupation	....	....	....
	....	....	....
Religion	....	....	....
Date of Marriage(s)	....	....	....
	....	....	....
	....	....	....
Date of Death	....	....	....
Place of Burial	....	....	....

GREAT-GRANDFATHER'S BROTHERS (GREAT-GREAT-UNCLES)

Surname	....	....	....
Given Name(s)	....	....	....
	....	....	....
Nationality	....	....	....
Date of Birth	....	....	....
Place of Birth	....	....	....
	....	....	....
Home Address(es)	....	....	....
	....	....	....
	....	....	....
	....	....	....
Occupation	....	....	....
	....	....	....
Religion	....	....	....
Date of Marriage(s)	....	....	....
	....	....	....
	....	....	....
Date of Death	....	....	....
Place of Burial	....	....	....

GREAT-GRANDFATHER'S SISTERS (GREAT-GREAT-AUNTS)

Surname	....	....	....
Given Name(s)	....	....	....
	....	....	....
Nationality	....	....	....
Date of Birth	....	....	....
Place of Birth	....	....	....
	....	....	....
Home Address(es)	....	....	....
	....	....	....
	....	....	....
	....	....	....
Occupation	....	....	....
	....	....	....
Religion	....	....	....
Date of Marriage(s)	....	....	....
	....	....	....
Married Name	....	....	....
Date of Death	....	....	....
Place of Burial	....	....	....

GREAT-GRANDFATHER'S SISTERS (GREAT-GREAT-AUNTS)

Surname	. . . .	. . . .	. . . .
Given Name(s)	. . . .	. . . .	. . . .
	. . . .	. . . .	. . . .
Nationality	. . . .	. . . .	. . . .
Date of Birth	. . . .	. . . .	. . . .
Place of Birth	. . . .	. . . .	. . . .
	. . . .	. . . .	. . . .
Home Address(es)	. . . .	. . . .	. . . .
	. . . .	. . . .	. . . .
	. . . .	. . . .	. . . .
	. . . .	. . . .	. . . .
Occupation	. . . .	. . . .	. . . .
	. . . .	. . . .	. . . .
Religion	. . . .	. . . .	. . . .
Date of Marriage(s)	. . . .	. . . .	. . . .
	. . . .	. . . .	. . . .
Married Name	. . . .	. . . .	. . . .
Date of Death	. . . .	. . . .	. . . .
Place of Burial	. . . .	. . . .	. . . .

GREAT-GRANDMOTHER (FATHER'S FATHER'S MOTHER)

Surname . . . .　　Additional Information

Given Name(s) . . . .　　. . . . .

. . . .　　. . . . .

Nationality . . . .　　. . . . .

Date of Birth . . . .　　. . . . .

Place of Birth . . . .　　. . . . .

. . . .　　. . . . .

Home Address(s) . . . .　　. . . . .

. . . .　　. . . . .

. . . .　　. . . . .

. . . .　　. . . . .

Occupation . . . .　　. . . . .

. . . .　　. . . . .

Religion . . . .　　. . . . .

Date of Marriage(s) . . . .　　. . . . .

. . . .　　. . . . .

Married Name . . . .　　. . . . .

Date of Death . . . .　　. . . . .

Place of Burial . . . .　　. . . . .

GREAT-GRANDMOTHER BROTHERS (GREAT-GREAT-UNCLES)

Surname	....	....	....
Given Name(s)	....	....	....
	....	....	....
Nationality	....	....	....
Date of Birth	....	....	....
Place of Birth	....	....	....
	....	....	....
Home Address(es)	....	....	....
	....	....	....
	....	....	....
	....	....	....
Occupation	....	....	....
	....	....	....
Religion	....	....	....
Date of Marriage(s)	....	....	....
	....	....	....
	....	....	....
Date of Death	....	....	....
Place of Burial	....	....	....

GREAT-GRANDMOTHER'S BROTHERS (GREAT-GREAT-UNCLES)

Surname	....	....	....
Given Name(s)	....	....	....
	....	....	....
Nationality	....	....	....
Date of Birth	....	....	....
Place of Birth	....	....	....
	....	....	....
Home Address(es)	....	....	....
	....	....	....
	....	....	....
	....	....	....
Occupation	....	....	....
	....	....	....
Religion	....	....	....
Date of Marriage(s)	....	....	....
	....	....	....
	....	....	....
Date of Death	....	....	....
Place of Burial	....	....	....

GREAT-GRANDMOTHER'S SISTERS (GREAT-GREAT-AUNTS)

Surname	....	....	....
Given Name(s)	....	....	....
	....	....	....
Nationality	....	....	....
Date of Birth	....	....	....
Place of Birth	....	....	....
	....	....	....
Home Address(es)	....	....	....
	....	....	....
	....	....	....
	....	....	....
Occupation	....	....	....
	....	....	....
Religion	....	....	....
Date of Marriage(s)	....	....	....
	....	....	....
Married Name	....	....	....
Date of Death	....	....	....
Place of Burial	....	....	....

GREAT-GRANDMOTHER'S SISTERS (GREAT-GREAT-AUNTS)

Surname	....	....	....
Given Name(s)	....	....	....
	....	....	....
Nationality	....	....	....
Date of Birth	....	....	....
Place of Birth	....	....	....
	....	....	....
Home Address(es)	....	....	....
	....	....	....
	....	....	....
	....	....	....
Occupation	....	....	....
	....	....	....
Religion	....	....	....
Date of Marriage(s)	....	....	....
	....	....	....
Married Name	....	....	....
Date of Death	....	....	....
Place of Burial	....	....	....

GREAT-GRANDFATHER (FATHER'S MOTHER'S FATHER)

Surname .... Additional Information

Given Name(s) ....

....

Nationality ....

Date of Birth ....

Place of Birth ....

....

Home Address(es) ....

....

....

....

Occupation ....

....

Religion ....

Date of Marriage(s) ....

....

....

Date of Death ....

Place of Burial ....

GREAT-GRANDFATHER'S BROTHERS (GREAT-GREAT-UNCLES)

Surname	....	....	....
Given Name(s)	....	....	....
	....	....	....
Nationality	....	....	....
Date of Birth	....	....	....
Place of Birth	....	....	....
	....	....	....
Home Address(es)	....	....	....
	....	....	....
	....	....	....
	....	....	....
Occupation	....	....	....
	....	....	....
Religion	....	....	....
Date of Marriage(s)	....	....	....
	....	....	....
	....	....	....
Date of Death	....	....	....
Place of Burial	....	....	....

PATERNAL LINE
GREAT-GRANDFATHER'S BROTHERS (GREAT-GREAT-UNCLES)

Surname	....	....	....
Given Name(s)	....	....	....
	....	....	....
Nationality	....	....	....
Date of Birth	....	....	....
Place of Birth	....	....	....
	....	....	....
Home Address(es)	....	....	....
	....	....	....
	....	....	....
	....	....	....
Occupation	....	....	....
	....	....	....
Religion	....	....	....
Date of Marriage(s)	....	....	....
	....	....	....
	....	....	....
Date of Death	....	....	....
Place of Burial	....	....	....

GREAT-GRANDFATHER'S SISTERS (GREAT-GREAT-AUNTS)

Surname	....	....	....
Given Name(s)	....	....	....
	....	....	....
Nationality	....	....	....
Date of Birth	....	....	....
Place of Birth	....	....	....
	....	....	....
Home Address(es)	....	....	....
	....	....	....
	....	....	....
	....	....	....
Occupation	....	....	....
	....	....	....
Religion	....	....	....
Date of Marriage(s)	....	....	....
	....	....	....
Married Name	....	....	....
Date of Death	....	....	....
Place of Burial	....	....	....

GREAT-GRANDFATHER'S SISTERS (GREAT-GREAT-AUNTS)

Surname ....

Given Name(s) ....

....

Nationality ....

Date of Birth ....

Place of Birth ....

....

Home Address(es) ....

....

....

....

Occupation ....

....

Religion ....

Date of Marriage(s) ....

....

Married Name ....

Date of Death ....

Place of Burial ....

PATERNAL LINE

GREAT-GRANDMOTHER (FATHER'S MOTHER'S MOTHER)

Surname .... Additional Information

Given Name(s) ....

....

Nationality ....

Date of Birth ....

Place of Birth ....

....

Home Address(es) ....

....

....

....

Occupation ....

....

Religion ....

Date of Marriage(s) ....

....

Married Name ....

Date of Death ....

Place of Burial ....

GREAT-GRANDMOTHER'S BROTHERS (GREAT-GREAT-UNCLES)

Surname	....	....	....
Given Name(s)	....	....	....
	....	....	....
Nationality	....	....	....
Date of Birth	....	....	....
Place of Birth	....	....	....
	....	....	....
Home Address(es)	....	....	....
	....	....	....
	....	....	....
	....	....	....
Occupation	....	....	....
	....	....	....
Religion	....	....	....
Date of Marriage(s)	....	....	....
	....	....	....
	....	....	....
Date of Death	....	....	....
Place of Burial	....	....	....

GREAT-GRANDMOTHER'S BROTHERS (GREAT-GREAT-UNCLES)

Surname			
Given Name(s)			
Nationality			
Date of Birth			
Place of Birth			
Home Address(es)			
Occupation			
Religion			
Date of Marriage(s)			
Date of Death			
Place of Burial			

GREAT-GRANDMOTHER'S SISTERS (GREAT-GREAT-AUNTS)

Surname ....

Given Name(s) ....

....

Nationality ....

Date of Birth ....

Place of Birth ....

....

Home Address(es) ....

....

....

....

Occupation ....

....

Religion ....

Date of Marriage(s) ....

....

Married Name ....

Date of Death ....

Place of Burial ....

GREAT-GRANDMOTHER'S SISTERS (GREAT-GREAT-AUNTS)

Surname	....	....	....
Given Name(s)	....	....	....
	....	....	....
Nationality	....	....	....
Date of Birth	....	....	....
Place of Birth	....	....	....
	....	....	....
Home Address(es)	....	....	....
	....	....	....
	....	....	....
	....	....	....
Occupation	....	....	....
	....	....	....
Religion	....	....	....
Date of Marriage(s)	....	....	....
	....	....	....
Married Name	....	....	....
Date of Death	....	....	....
Place of Burial	....	....	....

ADDITIONAL INFORMATION

....

....

....

....

....

....

....

....

....

....

....

....

....

....

....

....

....

MOTHER

Surname	.... Additional Information
Given Name(s)	....
	....
Nationality	....
Date of Birth	....
Place of Birth	....
	....
Home Address(es)	....
	....
	....
	....
Occupation	....
	....
Religion	....
Date of Marriage(s)	....
	....
Married Name	....
Date of Death	....
Place of Burial	....

MATERNAL LINE

MOTHER'S BROTHERS (UNCLES)

Surname	....	....	....
Given Name(s)	....	....	....
	....	....	....
Nationality	....	....	....
Date of Birth	....	....	....
Place of Birth	....	....	....
	....	....	....
Home Address(es)	....	....	....
	....	....	....
	....	....	....
	....	....	....
Occupation	....	....	....
	....	....	....
Religion	....	....	....
Date of Marriage(s)	....	....	....
	....	....	....
	....	....	....
Date of Death	....	....	....
Place of Burial	....	....	....

MOTHER'S BROTHERS (UNCLES)

Surname	....	....	....
Given Name(s)	....	....	....
	....	....	....
Nationality	....	....	....
Date of Birth	....	....	....
Place of Birth	....	....	....
	....	....	....
Home Address(es)	....	....	....
	....	....	....
	....	....	....
	....	....	....
Occupation	....	....	....
	....	....	....
Religion	....	....	....
Date of Marriage(s)	....	....	....
	....	....	....
	....	....	....
Date of Death	....	....	....
Place of Burial	....	....	....

MATERNAL LINE

MOTHER'S BROTHERS' CHILDREN (FIRST COUSINS)

Surname . . . . Child of . . . .

Given Name(s) . . . . and . . . .

Surname . . . . Child of . . . .

Given Name(s) . . . . and . . . .

Surname . . . . Child of . . . .

Given Name(s) . . . . and . . . .

Surname . . . . Child of . . . .

Given Name(s) . . . . and . . . .

Surname . . . . Child of . . . .

Given Name(s) . . . . and . . . .

Surname . . . . Child of . . . .

Given Name(s) . . . . and . . . .

Surname . . . . Child of . . . .

Given Name(s) . . . . and . . . .

Surname . . . . Child of . . . .

Given Name(s) . . . . and . . . .

Surname . . . . Child of . . . .

Given Name(s) . . . . and . . . .

MATERNAL LINE

MOTHER'S BROTHERS' CHILDREN (FIRST COUSINS)

Surname . . . .

Given Name(s) . . . .

Surname . . . .

Given Name(s) . . . .

Surname . . . .

Given Name(s) . . . .

Surname . . . .

Given Name(s) . . . .

Surname . . . .

Given Name(s) . . . .

Surname . . . .

Given Name(s) . . . .

Surname . . . .

Given Name(s) . . . .

Surname . . . .

Given Name(s) . . . .

Child of . . . .

and . . . .

Child of . . . .

and . . . .

Child of . . . .

and . . . .

Child of . . . .

and . . . .

Child of . . . .

and . . . .

Child of . . . .

and . . . .

Child of . . . .

and . . . .

Child of . . . .

and . . . .

MOTHER'S SISTERS (AUNTS)

Surname	....	....	....
Given Name(s)	....	....	....
	....	....	....
Nationality	....	....	....
Date of Birth	....	....	....
Place of Birth	....	....	....
	....	....	....
Home Address(es)	....	....	....
	....	....	....
	....	....	....
	....	....	....
Occupation	....	....	....
	....	....	....
Religion	....	....	....
Date of Marriage(s)	....	....	....
	....	....	....
Married Name	....	....	....
Date of Death	....	....	....
Place of Burial	....	....	....

MOTHER'S SISTERS (AUNTS)

Surname	. . . .	. . . .	. . . .
Given Name(s)	. . . .	. . . .	. . . .
	. . . .	. . . .	. . . .
Nationality	. . . .	. . . .	. . . .
Date of Birth	. . . .	. . . .	. . . .
Place of Birth	. . . .	. . . .	. . . .
	. . . .	. . . .	. . . .
Home Address(es)	. . . .	. . . .	. . . .
	. . . .	. . . .	. . . .
	. . . .	. . . .	. . . .
	. . . .	. . . .	. . . .
Occupation	. . . .	. . . .	. . . .
	. . . .	. . . .	. . . .
Religion	. . . .	. . . .	. . . .
Date of Marriage(s)	. . . .	. . . .	. . . .
	. . . .	. . . .	. . . .
Married Name	. . . .	. . . .	. . . .
Date of Death	. . . .	. . . .	. . . .
Place of Burial	. . . .	. . . .	. . . .

MATERNAL LINE

MOTHER'S SISTERS' CHILDREN (FIRST COUSINS)

Surname	....	Child of	....
Given Name(s)	....	and	....
Surname	....	Child of	....
Given Name(s)	....	and	....
Surname	....	Child of	....
Given Name(s)	....	and	....
Surname	....	Child of	....
Given Name(s)	....	and	....
Surname	....	Child of	....
Given Name(s)	....	and	....
Surname	....	Child of	....
Given Name(s)	....	and	....
Surname	....	Child of	....
Given Name(s)	....	and	....
Surname	....	Child of	....
Given Name(s)	....	and	....

MATERNAL LINE

MOTHER'S SISTERS' CHILDREN (FIRST COUSINS)

Surname	....	Child of	....
Given Name(s)	....	and	....
Surname	....	Child of	....
Given Name(s)	....	and	....
Surname	....	Child of	....
Given Name(s)	....	and	....
Surname	....	Child of	....
Given Name(s)	....	and	....
Surname	....	Child of	....
Given Name(s)	....	and	....
Surname	....	Child of	....
Given Name(s)	....	and	....
Surname	....	Child of	....
Given Name(s)	....	and	....
Surname	....	Child of	....
Given Name(s)	....	and	....

ADDITIONAL INFORMATION

ADDITIONAL INFORMATION

....
....
....
....
....
....
....
....
....
....
....
....
....
....
....
....
....

MATERNAL LINE

GRANDFATHER (MOTHER'S FATHER)

Surname ....   Additional Information

Given Name(s) ....

....

Nationality ....

Date of Birth ....

Place of Birth ....

....

Home Address(es) ....

....

....

....

Occupation ....

....

Religion ....

Date of Marriage(s) ....

....

....

Date of Death ....

Place of Burial ....

GRANDFATHER'S BROTHERS (GREAT-UNCLES)

Surname	....	....	....
Given Name(s)	....	....	....
	....	....	....
Nationality	....	....	....
Date of Birth	....	....	....
Place of Birth	....	....	....
	....	....	....
Home Address(es)	....	....	....
	....	....	....
	....	....	....
	....	....	....
Occupation	....	....	....
	....	....	....
Religion	....	....	....
Date of Marriage(s)	....	....	....
	....	....	....
	....	....	....
Date of Death	....	....	....
Place of Burial	....	....	....

GRANDFATHER'S BROTHERS (GREAT-UNCLES)

Surname ....

Given Name(s) ....

....

Nationality ....

Date of Birth ....

Place of Birth ....

....

Home Address(es) ....

....

....

....

Occupation ....

....

Religion ....

Date of Marriage(s) ....

....

....

Date of Death ....

Place of Burial ....

MATERNAL LINE

GRANDFATHER'S BROTHERS' CHILDREN (FIRST COUSINS ONCE REMOVED)

Surname .... Child of ....

Given Name(s) .... and ....

Surname .... Child of ....

Given Name(s) .... and ....

Surname .... Child of ....

Given Name(s) .... and ....

Surname .... Child of ....

Given Name(s) .... and ....

Surname .... Child of ....

Given Name(s) .... and ....

Surname .... Child of ....

Given Name(s) .... and ....

Surname .... Child of ....

Given Name(s) .... and ....

Surname .... Child of ....

Given Name(s) .... and ....

Surname .... Child of ....

Given Name(s) .... and ....

GRANDFATHER'S SISTERS (GREAT-AUNTS)

Surname	....	....	....
Given Name(s)	....	....	....
	....	....	....
Nationality	....	....	....
Date of Birth	....	....	....
Place of Birth	....	....	....
	....	....	....
Home Address(es)	....	....	....
	....	....	....
	....	....	....
	....	....	....
Occupation	....	....	....
	....	....	....
Religion	....	....	....
Date of Marriage(s)	....	....	....
	....	....	....
Married Name	....	....	....
Date of Death	....	....	....
Place of Burial	....	....	....

GRANDFATHER'S SISTERS (GREAT-AUNTS)

Surname	. . . .	. . . .	. . . .
Given Name(s)	. . . .	. . . .	. . . .
	. . . .	. . . .	. . . .
Nationality	. . . .	. . . .	. . . .
Date of Birth	. . . .	. . . .	. . . .
Place of Birth	. . . .	. . . .	. . . .
	. . . .	. . . .	. . . .
Home Address(es)	. . . .	. . . .	. . . .
	. . . .	. . . .	. . . .
	. . . .	. . . .	. . . .
	. . . .	. . . .	. . . .
Occupation	. . . .	. . . .	. . . .
	. . . .	. . . .	. . . .
Religion	. . . .	. . . .	. . . .
Date of Marriage(s)	. . . .	. . . .	. . . .
	. . . .	. . . .	. . . .
Married Name	. . . .	. . . .	. . . .
Date of Death	. . . .	. . . .	. . . .
Place of Burial	. . . .	. . . .	. . . .

GRANDFATHER'S SISTERS' CHILDREN (FIRST COUSINS ONCE REMOVED)

Surname . . . .

Child of . . . .

Given Name(s) . . . .

and . . . .

Surname . . . .

Child of . . . .

Given Name(s) . . . .

and . . . .

Surname . . . .

Child of . . . .

Given Name(s) . . . .

and . . . .

Surname . . . .

Child of . . . .

Given Name(s) . . . .

and . . . .

Surname . . . .

Child of . . . .

Given Name(s) . . . .

and . . . .

Surname . . . .

Child of . . . .

Given Name(s) . . . .

and . . . .

Surname . . . .

Child of . . . .

Given Name(s) . . . .

and . . . .

Surname . . . .

Child of . . . .

Given Name(s) . . . .

and . . . .

MATERNAL LINE

GRANDMOTHER (MOTHER'S MOTHER)

Surname ....   Additional Information

Given Name(s) ....

....

Nationality ....

Date of Birth ....

Place of Birth ....

....

Home Address(es) ....

....

....

....

Occupation ....

....

Religion ....

Date of Marriage(s) ....

....

Married Name ....

Date of Death ....

Place of Burial ....

GRANDMOTHER'S BROTHERS (GREAT-UNCLES)

Surname	....	....	....
Given Name(s)	....	....	....
	....	....	....
Nationality	....	....	....
Date of Birth	....	....	....
Place of Birth	....	....	....
	....	....	....
Home Address(es)	....	....	....
	....	....	....
	....	....	....
	....	....	....
Occupation	....	....	....
	....	....	....
Religion	....	....	....
Date of Marriage(s)	....	....	....
	....	....	....
	....	....	....
Date of Death	....	....	....
Place of Burial	....	....	....

GRANDMOTHER'S BROTHERS (GREAT-UNCLES)

Surname	....	....	....
Given Name(s)	....	....	....
	....	....	....
Nationality	....	....	....
Date of Birth	....	....	....
Place of Birth	....	....	....
	....	....	....
Home Address(es)	....	....	....
	....	....	....
	....	....	....
	....	....	....
Occupation	....	....	....
	....	....	....
Religion	....	....	....
Date of Marriage(s)	....	....	....
	....	....	....
	....	....	....
Date of Death	....	....	....
Place of Burial	....	....	....

GRANDMOTHER'S BROTHERS' CHILDREN (FIRST COUSINS ONCE REMOVED)

Surname . . . . Child of . . . .

Given Name(s) . . . . and . . . .

Surname . . . . Child of . . . .

Given Name(s) . . . . and . . . .

Surname . . . . Child of . . . .

Given Name(s) . . . . and . . . .

Surname . . . . Child of . . . .

Given Name(s) . . . . and . . . .

Surname . . . . Child of . . . .

Given Name(s) . . . . and . . . .

Surname . . . . Child of . . . .

Given Name(s) . . . . and . . . .

Surname . . . . Child of . . . .

Given Name(s) . . . . and . . . .

Surname . . . . Child of . . . .

Given Name(s) . . . . and . . . .

MATERNAL LINE

GRANDMOTHER'S SISTERS (GREAT-AUNTS)

Surname ....

Given Name(s) ....

....

Nationality ....

Date of Birth ....

Place of Birth ....

....

Home Address(es) ....

....

....

....

Occupation ....

....

Religion ....

Date of Marriage(s) ....

....

Married Name ....

Date of Death ....

Place of Burial ....

GRANDMOTHER'S SISTERS (GREAT-AUNTS)

Surname	. . . .	. . . .	. . . .
Given Name(s)	. . . .	. . . .	. . . .
	. . . .	. . . .	. . . .
Nationality	. . . .	. . . .	. . . .
Date of Birth	. . . .	. . . .	. . . .
Place of Birth	. . . .	. . . .	. . . .
	. . . .	. . . .	. . . .
Home Address(es)	. . . .	. . . .	. . . .
	. . . .	. . . .	. . . .
	. . . .	. . . .	. . . .
	. . . .	. . . .	. . . .
Occupation	. . . .	. . . .	. . . .
	. . . .	. . . .	. . . .
Religion	. . . .	. . . .	. . . .
Date of Marriage(s)	. . . .	. . . .	. . . .
	. . . .	. . . .	. . . .
Married Name	. . . .	. . . .	. . . .
Date of Death	. . . .	. . . .	. . . .
Place of Burial	. . . .	. . . .	. . . .

GRANDMOTHER'S SISTERS' CHILDREN (FIRST COUSINS ONCE REMOVED)

Surname	....	Child of	....
Given Name(s)	....	and	....
Surname	....	Child of	....
Given Name(s)	....	and	....
Surname	....	Child of	....
Given Name(s)	....	and	....
Surname	....	Child of	....
Given Name(s)	....	and	....
Surname	....	Child of	....
Given Name(s)	....	and	....
Surname	....	Child of	....
Given Name(s)	....	and	....
Surname	....	Child of	....
Given Name(s)	....	and	....
Surname	....	Child of	....
Given Name(s)	....	and	....

ADDITIONAL INFORMATION

ADDITIONAL INFORMATION

GREAT-GRANDFATHER (MOTHER'S FATHER'S FATHER)

Surname . . . .   Additional Information

Given Name(s) . . . .

. . . .

Nationality . . . .

Date of Birth . . . .

Place of Birth . . . .

. . . .

Home Address(es) . . . .

. . . .

. . . .

. . . .

Occupation . . . .

. . . .

Religion . . . .

Date of Marriage(s) . . . .

. . . .

. . . .

Date of Death . . . .

Place of Burial . . . .

GREAT-GRANDFATHER'S BROTHERS (GREAT-GREAT-UNCLES)

Surname	....	....	....
Given Name(s)	....	....	....
	....	....	....
Nationality	....	....	....
Date of Birth	....	....	....
Place of Birth	....	....	....
	....	....	....
Home Address(es)	....	....	....
	....	....	....
	....	....	....
	....	....	....
Occupation	....	....	....
	....	....	....
Religion	....	....	....
Date of Marriage(s)	....	....	....
	....	....	....
	....	....	....
Date of Death	....	....	....
Place of Burial	....	....	....

GREAT-GRANDFATHER'S BROTHERS (GREAT-GREAT-UNCLES)

Surname	....	....	....
Given Name(s)	....	....	....
	....	....	....
Nationality	....	....	....
Date of Birth	....	....	....
Place of Birth	....	....	....
	....	....	....
Home Address(es)	....	....	....
	....	....	....
	....	....	....
	....	....	....
Occupation	....	....	....
	....	....	....
Religion	....	....	....
Date of Marriage(s)	....	....	....
	....	....	....
	....	....	....
Date of Death	....	....	....
Place of Burial	....	....	....

GREAT-GRANDFATHER'S SISTERS (GREAT-GREAT-AUNTS)

Surname	....	....	....
Given Name(s)	....	....	....
	....	....	....
Nationality	....	....	....
Date of Birth	....	....	....
Place of Birth	....	....	....
	....	....	....
Home Address(es)	....	....	....
	....	....	....
	....	....	....
	....	....	....
Occupation	....	....	....
	....	....	....
Religion	....	....	....
Date of Marriage(s)	....	....	....
	....	....	....
Married Name	....	....	....
Date of Death	....	....	....
Place of Burial	....	....	....

GREAT-GRANDFATHER'S SISTERS (GREAT-GREAT-AUNTS)

Surname	....	....	....
Given Name(s)	....	....	....
	....	....	....
Nationality	....	....	....
Date of Birth	....	....	....
Place of Birth	....	....	....
	....	....	....
Home Address(es)	....	....	....
	....	....	....
	....	....	....
	....	....	....
Occupation	....	....	....
	....	....	....
Religion	....	....	....
Date of Marriage(s)	....	....	....
	....	....	....
Married Name	....	....	....
Date of Death	....	....	....
Place of Burial	....	....	....

GREAT-GRANDMOTHER (MOTHER'S FATHER'S MOTHER)

Surname	. . . .
	Additional Information
Given Name(s)	. . . .
	. . . .
	. . . .
	. . . .
Nationality	. . . .
	. . . .
Date of Birth	. . . .
	. . . .
Place of Birth	. . . .
	. . . .
	. . . .
Home Address(es)	. . . .
	. . . .
	. . . .
	. . . .
	. . . .
	. . . .
Occupation	. . . .
	. . . .
	. . . .
Religion	. . . .
Date of Marriage(s)	. . . .
	. . . .
Married Name	. . . .
Date of Death	. . . .
Place of Burial	. . . .

GREAT-GRANDMOTHER'S BROTHERS (GREAT-GREAT-UNCLES)

Surname ....

Given Name(s) ....

....

Nationality ....

Date of Birth ....

Place of Birth ....

....

Home Address(es) ....

....

....

....

Occupation ....

....

Religion ....

Date of Marriage(s) ....

....

....

Date of Death ....

Place of Burial ....

GREAT-GRANDMOTHER'S BROTHERS (GREAT-GREAT-UNCLES)

Surname	....	....	....
Given Name(s)	....	....	....
	....	....	....
Nationality	....	....	....
Date of Birth	....	....	....
Place of Birth	....	....	....
	....	....	....
Home Address(es)	....	....	....
	....	....	....
	....	....	....
	....	....	....
Occupation	....	....	....
	....	....	....
Religion	....	....	....
Date of Marriage(s)	....	....	....
	....	....	....
	....	....	....
Date of Death	....	....	....
Place of Burial	....	....	....

MATERNAL LINE

GREAT-GRANDMOTHER'S SISTERS (GREAT-GREAT-AUNTS)

Surname	....	....	....
Given Name(s)	....	....	....
	....	....	....
Nationality	....	....	....
Date of Birth	....	....	....
Place of Birth	....	....	....
	....	....	....
Home Address(es)	....	....	....
	....	....	....
	....	....	....
	....	....	....
Occupation	....	....	....
	....	....	....
Religion	....	....	....
Date of Marriage(s)	....	....	....
	....	....	....
Married Name	....	....	....
Date of Death	....	....	....
Place of Burial	....	....	....

GREAT-GRANDMOTHER'S SISTERS (GREAT-GREAT-AUNTS)

Surname	. . . .	. . . .	. . . .
Given Name(s)	. . . .	. . . .	. . . .
	. . . .	. . . .	. . . .
Nationality	. . . .	. . . .	. . . .
Date of Birth	. . . .	. . . .	. . . .
Place of Birth	. . . .	. . . .	. . . .
	. . . .	. . . .	. . . .
Home Address(es)	. . . .	. . . .	. . . .
	. . . .	. . . .	. . . .
	. . . .	. . . .	. . . .
	. . . .	. . . .	. . . .
Occupation	. . . .	. . . .	. . . .
	. . . .	. . . .	. . . .
Religion	. . . .	. . . .	. . . .
Date of Marriage(s)	. . . .	. . . .	. . . .
	. . . .	. . . .	. . . .
Married Name	. . . .	. . . .	. . . .
Date of Death	. . . .	. . . .	. . . .
Place of Burial	. . . .	. . . .	. . . .

GREAT-GRANDFATHER (MOTHER'S MOTHER'S FATHER)

Surname .... Additional Information

Given Name(s) ....

....

Nationality ....

Date of Birth ....

Place of Birth ....

....

Home Address(es) ....

....

....

....

Occupation ....

....

Religion ....

Date of Marriage(s) ....

....

....

Date of Death ....

Place of Burial ....

GREAT-GRANDFATHER'S BROTHERS (GREAT-GREAT-UNCLES)

Surname	....	....	....
Given Name(s)	....	....	....
	....	....	....
Nationality	....	....	....
Date of Birth	....	....	....
Place of Birth	....	....	....
	....	....	....
Home Address(es)	....	....	....
	....	....	....
	....	....	....
	....	....	....
Occupation	....	....	....
	....	....	....
Religion	....	....	....
Date of Marriage(s)	....	....	....
	....	....	....
	....	....	....
Date of Death	....	....	....
Place of Burial	....	....	....

GREAT-GRANDFATHER'S BROTHERS (GREAT-GREAT-UNCLES)

Surname	....	....	....
Given Name(s)	....	....	....
	....	....	....
Nationality	....	....	....
Date of Birth	....	....	....
Place of Birth	....	....	....
	....	....	....
Home Address(es)	....	....	....
	....	....	....
	....	....	....
	....	....	....
Occupation	....	....	....
	....	....	....
Religion	....	....	....
Date of Marriage(s)	....	....	....
	....	....	....
	....	....	....
Date of Death	....	....	....
Place of Burial	....	....	....

GREAT-GRANDFATHER'S SISTERS (GREAT-GREAT-AUNTS)

Surname	....	....	....
Given Name(s)	....	....	....
	....	....	....
Nationality	....	....	....
Date of Birth	....	....	....
Place of Birth	....	....	....
	....	....	....
Home Address(es)	....	....	....
	....	....	....
	....	....	....
Occupation	....	....	....
	....	....	....
Religion	....	....	....
Date of Marriage(s)	....	....	....
	....	....	....
Married Name	....	....	....
Date of Death	....	....	....
Place of Burial	....	....	....

GREAT-GRANDFATHER'S SISTERS (GREAT-GREAT-AUNTS)

Surname	....	....	....
Given Name(s)	....	....	....
	....	....	....
Nationality	....	....	....
Date of Birth	....	....	....
Place of Birth	....	....	....
	....	....	....
Home Address(es)	....	....	....
	....	....	....
	....	....	....
	....	....	....
Occupation	....	....	....
	....	....	....
Religion	....	....	....
Date of Marriage(s)	....	....	....
	....	....	....
Married Name	....	....	....
Date of Death	....	....	....
Place of Burial	....	....	....

GREAT-GRANDMOTHER (MOTHER'S MOTHER'S MOTHER)

Surname .... Additional Information

Given Name(s) ....

....

Nationality ....

Date of Birth ....

Place of Birth ....

....

Home Address(es) ....

....

....

....

Occupation ....

....

Religion ....

Date of Marriage(s) ....

....

Married Name ....

Date of Death ....

Place of Burial ....

GREAT-GRANDMOTHER'S BROTHERS (GREAT-GREAT-UNCLES)

Surname	....	....	....
Given Name(s)	....	....	....
	....	....	....
Nationality	....	....	....
Date of Birth	....	....	....
Place of Birth	....	....	....
	....	....	....
Home Address(es)	....	....	....
	....	....	....
	....	....	....
	....	....	....
Occupation	....	....	....
	....	....	....
Religion	....	....	....
Date of Marriage(s)	....	....	....
	....	....	....
	....	....	....
Date of Death	....	....	....
Place of Burial	....	....	....

GREAT-GRANDMOTHER'S BROTHERS (GREAT-GREAT-UNCLES)

Surname	....	....	....
Given Name(s)	....	....	....
	....	....	....
Nationality	....	....	....
Date of Birth	....	....	....
Place of Birth	....	....	....
	....	....	....
Home Address(es)	....	....	....
	....	....	....
	....	....	....
	....	....	....
Occupation	....	....	....
	....	....	....
Religion	....	....	....
Date of Marriage(s)	....	....	....
	....	....	....
	....	....	....
Date of Death	....	....	....
Place of Burial	....	....	....

MATERNAL LINE

GREAT-GRANDMOTHER'S SISTERS (GREAT-GREAT-AUNTS)

Surname	....	....	....
Given Name(s)	....	....	....
	....	....	....
Nationality	....	....	....
Date of Birth	....	....	....
Place of Birth	....	....	....
	....	....	....
Home Address(es)	....	....	....
	....	....	....
	....	....	....
	....	....	....
Occupation	....	....	....
	....	....	....
Religion	....	....	....
Date of Marriage(s)	....	....	....
	....	....	....
Married Name	....	....	....
Date of Death	....	....	....
Place of Burial	....	....	....

GREAT-GRANDMOTHER'S SISTERS (GREAT-GREAT-AUNTS)

Surname	....	....	....
Given Name(s)	....	....	....
	....	....	....
Nationality	....	....	....
Date of Birth	....	....	....
Place of Birth	....	....	....
	....	....	....
Home Address(es)	....	....	....
	....	....	....
	....	....	....
	....	....	....
Occupation	....	....	....
	....	....	....
Religion	....	....	....
Date of Marriage(s)	....	....	....
	....	....	....
Married Name	....	....	....
Date of Death	....	....	....
Place of Burial	....	....	....

ADDITIONAL INFORMATION

FEMALE COMPILER'S CHART

PATERNAL LINE

GREAT GREAT GRANDPARENTS	GREAT GRANDPARENTS	GRAND PARENTS	FATHER

....
....

....
....

....
....

....

....

....

....

....

....

....

....

....

....

....

....

....

....

....

....

....

FEM.

....

....

....

....

....

....

....

....

....

....

....

....

....

....

FEMALE COMPILER'S CHART

MOTHER	GRAND PARENTS	GREAT GRANDPARENTS	GREAT GREAT GRANDPARENTS
			. . . .
			. . . .
		. . . .	
		. . . .	. . . .
	. . . .		. . . .
			. . . .
	. . . .		. . . .
		. . . .	. . . .
		. . . .	. . . .
			. . . .
. . . .			. . . .
. . . .			. . . .
		. . . .	. . . .
		. . . .	
	. . . .		. . . .
	. . . .		. . . .
		. . . .	. . . .
. . . .		. . . .	
			. . . .
. . . .			. . . .

PILER

111

BRIEF BIOGRAPHY

Surname ....   Additional Information

Given Name(s) ....

Nationality ....

Date of Birth ....

Place of Birth ....

....

Marital Status ....

Religion ....

Occupation ....

....

Height/Weight ....

Colour of Hair/Eyes ....

Schools ....

....

....

Achievements ....

....

....

....

FATHER

		Additional Information
Surname	....	
Given Name(s)	....	....
	....	....
Nationality	....	....
Date of Birth	....	....
Place of Birth	....	....
	....	....
Home Address(es)	....	....
	....	....
	....	....
	....	....
Occupation	....	....
	....	....
Religion	....	....
Date of Marriage(s)	....	....
	....	....
Date of Death	....	....
Place of Burial	....	....

PATERNAL LINE

FATHER'S BROTHERS (UNCLES)

Surname	....	....	....
Given Name(s)	....	....	....
	....	....	....
Nationality	....	....	....
Date of Birth	....	....	....
Place of Birth	....	....	....
	....	....	....
Home Address(es)	....	....	....
	....	....	....
	....	....	....
	....	....	....
Occupation	....	....	....
	....	....	....
Religion	....	....	....
Date of Marriage(s)	....	....	....
	....	....	....
Date of Death	....	....	....
Place of Burial	....	....	....
	....	....	....

FATHER'S BROTHERS (UNCLES)

Surname	....	....	....
Given Name(s)	....	....	....
	....	....	....
Nationality	....	....	....
Date of Birth	....	....	....
Place of Birth	....	....	....
	....	....	....
Home Address(es)	....	....	....
	....	....	....
	....	....	....
	....	....	....
Occupation	....	....	....
	....	....	....
Religion	....	....	....
Date of Marriage(s)	....	....	....
	....	....	....
Date of Death	....	....	....
Place of Burial	....	....	....
	....	....	....

FATHER'S BROTHERS' CHILDREN (FIRST COUSINS)

Surname	....	Child of	....
Given Name(s)	....	and	....
Surname	....	Child of	....
Given Name(s)	....	and	....
Surname	....	Child of	....
Given Name(s)	....	and	....
Surname	....	Child of	....
Given Name(s)	....	and	....
Surname	....	Child of	....
Given Name(s)	....	and	....
Surname	....	Child of	....
Given Name(s)	....	and	....
Surname	....	Child of	....
Given Name(s)	....	and	....
Surname	....	Child of	....
Given Name(s)	....	and	....

FATHER'S BROTHERS' CHILDREN (FIRST COUSINS)

Surname . . . .

Given Name(s) . . . .

Surname . . . .

Given Name(s) . . . .

Surname . . . .

Given Name(s) . . . .

Surname . . . .

Given Name(s) . . . .

Surname . . . .

Given Name(s) . . . .

Surname . . . .

Given Name(s) . . . .

Surname . . . .

Given Name(s) . . . .

Surname . . . .

Given Name(s) . . . .

Child of . . . .

and . . . .

Child of . . . .

and . . . .

Child of . . . .

and . . . .

Child of . . . .

and . . . .

Child of . . . .

and . . . .

Child of . . . .

and . . . .

Child of . . . .

and . . . .

Child of . . . .

and . . . .

FATHER'S SISTERS (AUNTS)

Surname	....	....	....
Given Name(s)	....	....	....
	....	....	....
Nationality	....	....	....
Date of Birth	....	....	....
Place of Birth	....	....	....
	....	....	....
Home Address(es)	....	....	....
	....	....	....
	....	....	....
	....	....	....
Occupation	....	....	....
	....	....	....
Religion	....	....	....
Date of Marriage(s)	....	....	....
	....	....	....
Married Name	....	....	....
Date of Death	....	....	....
Place of Burial	....	....	....

FATHER'S SISTERS (AUNTS)

Surname	. . . .	. . . .	. . . .
Given Name(s)	. . . .	. . . .	. . . .
	. . . .	. . . .	. . . .
Nationality	. . . .	. . . .	. . . .
Date of Birth	. . . .	. . . .	. . . .
Place of Birth	. . . .	. . . .	. . . .
	. . . .	. . . .	. . . .
Home Address(es)	. . . .	. . . .	. . . .
	. . . .	. . . .	. . . .
	. . . .	. . . .	. . . .
	. . . .	. . . .	. . . .
Occupation	. . . .	. . . .	. . . .
	. . . .	. . . .	. . . .
Religion	. . . .	. . . .	. . . .
Date of Marriage(s)	. . . .	. . . .	. . . .
	. . . .	. . . .	. . . .
Married Name	. . . .	. . . .	. . . .
Date of Death	. . . .	. . . .	. . . .
Place of Burial	. . . .	. . . .	. . . .

FATHER'S SISTERS' CHILDREN (FIRST COUSINS)

Surname	....	Child of	....
Given Name(s)	....	and	....
Surname	....	Child of	....
Given Name(s)	....	and	....
Surname	....	Child of	....
Given Name(s)	....	and	....
Surname	....	Child of	....
Given Name(s)	....	and	....
Surname	....	Child of	....
Given Name(s)	....	and	....
Surname	....	Child of	....
Given Name(s)	....	and	....
Surname	....	Child of	....
Given Name(s)	....	and	....
Surname	....	Child of	....
Given Name(s)	....	and	....

FATHER'S SISTERS' CHILDREN (FIRST COUSINS)

Surname	....	Child of	....
Given Name(s)	....	and	....
Surname	....	Child of	....
Given Name(s)	....	and	....
Surname	....	Child of	....
Given Name(s)	....	and	....
Surname	....	Child of	....
Given Name(s)	....	and	....
Surname	....	Child of	....
Given Name(s)	....	and	....
Surname	....	Child of	....
Given Name(s)	....	and	....
Surname	....	Child of	....
Given Name(s)	....	and	....
Surname	....	Child of	....
Given Name(s)	....	and	....
Surname	....	Child of	....
Given Name(s)	....	and	....

....
....
....
....
....
....
....
....
....
....
....
....
....
....
....
....
....

....
....
....
....
....
....
....
....
....
....
....
....
....
....
....
....

PATERNAL LINE

GRANDFATHER (FATHER'S FATHER)

Surname . . . .   Additional Information

Given Name(s) . . . .

. . . .

Nationality . . . .

Date of Birth . . . .

Place of Birth . . . .

. . . .

Home Address(es) . . . .

. . . .

. . . .

. . . .

Occupation . . . .

. . . .

Religion . . . .

Date of Marriage(s) . . . .

. . . .

Date of Death . . . .

Place of Burial . . . .

. . . .

PATERNAL LINE

GRANDFATHER'S BROTHERS (GREAT-UNCLES)

Surname	....	....	....
Given Name(s)	....	....	....
	....	....	....
Nationality	....	....	....
Date of Birth	....	....	....
Place of Birth	....	....	....
	....	....	....
Home Address(es)	....	....	....
	....	....	....
	....	....	....
	....	....	....
Occupation	....	....	....
	....	....	....
Religion	....	....	....
Date of Marriage(s)	....	....	....
	....	....	....
Date of Death	....	....	....
Place of Burial	....	....	....
	....	....	....

GRANDFATHER'S BROTHERS (GREAT-UNCLES)

Surname	....	....	....
Given Name(s)	....	....	....
	....	....	....
Nationality	....	....	....
Date of Birth	....	....	....
Place of Birth	....	....	....
	....	....	....
Home Address(es)	....	....	....
	....	....	....
	....	....	....
	....	....	....
Occupation	....	....	....
	....	....	....
Religion	....	....	....
Date of Marriage(s)	....	....	....
	....	....	....
Date of Death	....	....	....
Place of Burial	....	....	....
	....	....	....

GRANDFATHER'S BROTHERS' CHILDREN (FIRST COUSINS ONCE REMOVED)

Surname	....	Child of	....
Given Name(s)	....	and	....
Surname	....	Child of	....
Given Name(s)	....	and	....
Surname	....	Child of	....
Given Name(s)	....	and	....
Surname	....	Child of	....
Given Name(s)	....	and	....
Surname	....	Child of	....
Given Name(s)	....	and	....
Surname	....	Child of	....
Given Name(s)	....	and	....
Surname	....	Child of	....
Given Name(s)	....	and	....
Surname	....	Child of	....
Given Name(s)	....	and	....

GRANDFATHER'S SISTERS (GREAT-AUNTS)

Surname	....	....	....
Given Name(s)	....	....	....
	....	....	....
Nationality	....	....	....
Date of Birth	....	....	....
Place of Birth	....	....	....
	....	....	....
Home Address(es)	....	....	....
	....	....	....
	....	....	....
	....	....	....
Occupation	....	....	....
	....	....	....
Religion	....	....	....
Date of Marriage(s)	....	....	....
	....	....	....
Married Name	....	....	....
Date of Death	....	....	....
Place of Burial	....	....	....

GRANDFATHER'S SISTERS (GREAT-AUNTS)

Surname	....	....	....
Given Name(s)	....	....	....
	....	....	....
Nationality	....	....	....
Date of Birth	....	....	....
Place of Birth	....	....	....
	....	....	....
Home Address(es)	....	....	....
	....	....	....
	....	....	....
	....	....	....
Occupation	....	....	....
	....	....	....
Religion	....	....	....
Date of Marriage(s)	....	....	....
	....	....	....
Married Name	....	....	....
Date of Death	....	....	....
Place of Burial	....	....	....

GRANDFATHER'S SISTERS' CHILDREN (FIRST COUSINS ONCE REMOVED)

Surname ....

Given Name(s) ....

Surname ....

Given Name(s) ....

Surname ....,

Given Name(s) ....

Surname ....

Given Name(s) ....

Surname ....

Given Name(s) ....

Surname ....

Given Name(s) ....

Surname ....

Given Name(s) ....

Surname ....

Given Name(s) ....

Child of ....

and ....

Child of ....

and ....

Child of ....

and ....

Child of ....

and ....

Child of ....

and ....

Child of ....

and ....

Child of ....

and ....

Child of ....

and ....

GRANDMOTHER (FATHER'S MOTHER)

Surname .... Additional Information

Given Name(s) ....

....

Nationality ....

Date of Birth ....

Place of Birth ....

....

Home Address(es) ....

....

....

....

Occupation ....

....

Religion ....

Date of Marriage(s) ....

....

Married Name ....

Date of Death ....

Place of Burial ....

GRANDMOTHER'S BROTHERS (GREAT-UNCLES)

Surname	....	....	....
Given Name(s)	....	....	....
	....	....	....
Nationality	....	....	....
Date of Birth	....	....	....
Place of Birth	....	....	....
	....	....	....
Home Address(es)	....	....	....
	....	....	....
	....	....	....
	....	....	....
Occupation	....	....	....
	....	....	....
Religion	....	....	....
Date of Marriage(s)	....	....	....
	....	....	....
Date of Death	....	....	....
Place of Burial	....	....	....

GRANDMOTHER'S BROTHERS (GREAT-UNCLES)

Surname	....	....	....
Given Name(s)	....	....	....
	....	....	....
Nationality	....	....	....
Date of Birth	....	....	....
Place of Birth	....	....	....
	....	....	....
Home Address(es)	....	....	....
	....	....	....
	....	....	....
	....	....	....
Occupation	....	....	....
	....	....	....
Religion	....	....	....
Date of Marriage(s)	....	....	....
	....	....	....
Date of Death	....	....	....
Place of Burial	....	....	....
	....	....	....

GRANDMOTHER'S BROTHERS' CHILDREN (FIRST COUSINS ONCE REMOVED)

Surname ....   Child of ....

Given Name(s) ....   and ....

Surname ....   Child of ....

Given Name(s) ....   and ....

Surname ....   Child of ....

Given Name(s) ....   and ....

Surname ....   Child of ....

Given Name(s) ....   and ....

Surname ....   Child of ....

Given Name(s) ....   and ....

Surname ....   Child of ....

Given Name(s) ....   and ....

Surname ....   Child of ....

Given Name(s) ....   and ....

Surname ....   Child of ....

Given Name(s) ....   and ....

GRANDMOTHER'S SISTERS (GREAT-AUNTS)

Surname	. . . .	. . . .	. . . .
Given Name(s)	. . . .	. . . .	. . . .
	. . . .	. . . .	. . . .
Nationality	. . . .	. . . .	. . . .
Date of Birth	. . . .	. . . .	. . . .
Place of Birth	. . . .	. . . .	. . . .
	. . . .	. . . .	. . . .
Home Address(es)	. . . .	. . . .	. . . .
	. . . .	. . . .	. . . .
	. . . .	. . . .	. . . .
Occupation	. . . .	. . . .	. . . .
	. . . .	. . . .	. . . .
Religion	. . . .	. . . .	. . . .
Date of Marriage(s)	. . . .	. . . .	. . . .
Married Name	. . . .	. . . .	. . . .
Date of Death	. . . .	. . . .	. . . .
Place of Burial	. . . .	. . . .	. . . .

GRANDMOTHER'S SISTERS (GREAT-AUNTS)

Surname	....	....	....
Given Name(s)	....	....	....
	....	....	....
Nationality	....	....	....
Date of Birth	....	....	....
Place of Birth	....	....	....
	....	....	....
Home Address(es)	....	....	....
	....	....	....
	....	....	....
	....	....	....
Occupation	....	....	....
	....	....	....
Religion	....	....	....
Date of Marriage(s)	....	....	....
	....	....	....
Married Name	....	....	....
Date of Death	....	....	....
Place of Burial	....	....	....

GRANDMOTHER'S SISTERS' CHILDREN (FIRST COUSINS ONCE REMOVED)

Surname	....	Child of	....
Given Name(s)	....	and	....
Surname	....	Child of	....
Given Name(s)	....	and	....
Surname	....	Child of	....
Given Name(s)	....	and	....
Surname	....	Child of	....
Given Name(s)	....	and	....
Surname	....	Child of	....
Given Name(s)	....	and	....
Surname	....	Child of	....
Given Name(s)	....	and	....
Surname	....	Child of	....
Given Name(s)	....	and	....
Surname	....	Child of	....
Given Name(s)	....	and	....

....

....

....

....

....

....

....

....

....

....

....

....

....

....

....

....

....

ADDITIONAL INFORMATION

GREAT-GRANDFATHER (FATHER'S FATHER'S FATHER)

Surname .... Additional Information

Given Name(s) ....

....

Nationality ....

Date of Birth ....

Place of Birth ....

....

Home Address(es) ....

....

....

....

Occupation ....

....

Religion ....

Date of Marriage(s) ....

....

Date of Death ....

Place of Burial ....

....

GREAT-GRANDFATHER'S BROTHERS (GREAT-GREAT-UNCLES)

Surname . . . .

Given Name(s) . . . .

. . . .

Nationality . . . .

Date of Birth . . . .

Place of Birth . . . .

. . . .

Home Address(es) . . . .

. . . .

. . . .

. . . .

Occupation . . . .

. . . .

Religion . . . .

Date of Marriage(s) . . . .

. . . .

Date of Death . . . .

Place of Burial . . . .

. . . .

GREAT-GRANDFATHER'S BROTHERS (GREAT-GREAT-UNCLES)

Surname	....	....	....
Given Name(s)	....	....	....
	....	....	....
Nationality	....	....	....
Date of Birth	....	....	....
Place of Birth	....	....	....
	....	....	....
Home Address(es)	....	....	....
	....	....	....
	....	....	....
	....	....	....
Occupation	....	....	....
	....	....	....
Religion	....	....	....
Date of Marriage(s)	....	....	....
	....	....	....
	....	....	....
Date of Death	....	....	....
Place of Burial	....	....	....

GREAT-GRANDFATHER'S SISTERS (GREAT-GREAT-AUNTS)

Surname	....	....	....
Given Name(s)	....	....	....
	....	....	....
Nationality	....	....	....
Date of Birth	....	....	....
Place of Birth	....	....	....
	....	....	....
Home Address(es)	....	....	....
	....	....	....
	....	....	....
	....	....	....
Occupation	....	....	....
	....	....	....
Religion	....	....	....
Date of Marriage(s)	....	....	....
	....	....	....
Married Name	....	....	....
Date of Death	....	....	....
Place of Burial	....	....	....

GREAT-GRANDFATHER'S SISTERS (GREAT-GREAT-AUNTS)

Surname	....	....	....
Given Name(s)	....	....	....
	....	....	....
Nationality	....	....	....
Date of Birth	....	....	....
Place of Birth	....	....	....
	....	....	....
Home Address(es)	....	....	....
	....	....	....
	....	....	....
	....	....	....
Occupation	....	....	....
	....	....	....
Religion	....	....	....
Date of Marriage(s)	....	....	....
	....	....	....
Married Name	....	....	....
Date of Death	....	....	....
Place of Burial	....	....	....

GREAT-GRANDMOTHER (FATHER'S FATHER'S MOTHER)

Surname .... Additional Information

Given Name(s) ....

....

Nationality ....

Date of Birth ....

Place of Birth ....

....

Home Address(es) ....

....

....

....

Occupation ....

....

Religion ....

Date of Marriage(s) ....

....

Married Name ....

Date of Death ....

Place of Burial ....

GREAT-GRANDMOTHER'S BROTHERS (GREAT-GREAT-UNCLES)

Surname			
Given Name(s)			
Nationality			
Date of Birth			
Place of Birth			
Home Address(es)			
Occupation			
Religion			
Date of Marriage(s)			
Date of Death			
Place of Burial			

GREAT-GRANDMOTHER'S BROTHERS (GREAT-GREAT-UNCLES)

Surname ....

Given Name(s) ....

....

Nationality ....

Date of Birth ....

Place of Birth ....

....

Home Address(es) ....

....

....

....

Occupation ....

....

Religion ....

Date of Marriage(s) ....

....

Date of Death ....

Place of Burial ....

....

GREAT-GRANDMOTHER'S SISTERS (GREAT-GREAT-AUNTS)

Surname	....	....	....
Given Name(s)	....	....	....
	....	....	....
Nationality	....	....	....
Date of Birth	....	....	....
Place of Birth	....	....	....
	....	....	....
Home Address(es)	....	....	....
	....	....	....
	....	....	....
	....	....	....
Occupation	....	....	....
	....	....	....
Religion	....	....	....
Date of Marriage(s)	....	....	....
	....	....	....
Married Name	....	....	....
Date of Death	....	....	....
Place of Burial	....	....	....

GREAT-GRANDMOTHER'S SISTERS (GREAT-GREAT-AUNTS)

Surname	....	....	....
Given Name(s)	....	....	....
	....	....	....
Nationality	....	....	....
Date of Birth	....	....	....
Place of Birth	....	....	....
	....	....	....
Home Address(es)	....	....	....
	....	....	....
	....	....	....
	....	....	....
Occupation	....	....	....
	....	....	....
Religion	....	....	....
Date of Marriage(s)	....	....	....
	....	....	....
Married Name	....	....	....
Date of Death	....	....	....
Place of Burial	....	....	....

GREAT-GRANDFATHER (FATHER'S MOTHER'S FATHER)

Surname . . . .   Additional Information

Given Name(s) . . . .

. . . .

Nationality . . . .

Date of Birth . . . .

Place of Birth . . . .

. . . .

Home Address(es) . . . .

. . . .

. . . .

. . . .

Occupation . . . .

. . . .

Religion . . . .

Date of Marriage(s) . . . .

. . . .

Date of Death . . . .

Place of Burial . . . .

. . . .

GREAT-GRANDFATHER'S BROTHERS (GREAT-GREAT-UNCLES)

Surname ....

Given Name(s) ....

....

Nationality ....

Date of Birth ....

Place of Birth ....

....

Home Address(es) ....

....

....

....

Occupation ....

....

Religion ....

Date of Marriage(s) ....

....

Date of Death ....

Place of Burial ....

....

GREAT-GRANDFATHER'S BROTHERS (GREAT-GREAT-UNCLES)

Surname ....

Given Name(s) ....

....

Nationality ....

Date of Birth ....

Place of Birth ....

....

Home Address(es) ....

....

....

....

Occupation ....

....

Religion ....

Date of Marriage(s) ....

....

Date of Death ....

Place of Burial ....

GREAT-GRANDFATHER'S SISTERS (GREAT-GREAT-AUNTS)

Surname	....	....	....
Given Name(s)	....	....	....
	....	....	....
Nationality	....	....	....
Date of Birth	....	....	....
Place of Birth	....	....	....
	....	....	....
Home Address(es)	....	....	....
	....	....	....
	....	....	....
	....	....	....
Occupation	....	....	....
	....	....	....
Religion	....	....	....
Date of Marriage(s)	....	....	....
	....	....	....
Married Name	....	....	....
Date of Burial	....	....	....
Place of Burial	....	....	....

GREAT-GRANDFATHER'S SISTERS (GREAT-GREAT-AUNTS)

Surname	....	....	....
Given Name(s)	....	....	....
	....	....	....
Nationality	....	....	....
Date of Birth	....	....	....
Place of Birth	....	....	....
	....	....	....
Home Address(es)	....	....	....
	....	....	....
	....	....	....
	....	....	....
Occupation	....	....	....
	....	....	....
Religion	....	....	....
Date of Marriage(s)	....	....	....
	....	....	....
Married Name	....	....	....
Date of Death	....	....	....
Place of Burial	....	....	....

GREAT-GRANDMOTHER (FATHER'S MOTHER'S MOTHER)

Surname .... Additional Information

Given Name(s) ....

....

Nationality ....

Date of Birth ....

Place of Birth ....

....

Home Address(es) ....

....

....

....

Occupation ....

....

Religion ....

Date of Marriage(s) ....

....

Married Name ....

Date of Death ....

Place of Burial ....

GREAT-GRANDMOTHER'S BROTHERS (GREAT-GREAT-UNCLES)

Surname ....

Given Name(s) ....

....

Nationality ....

Date of Birth ....

Place of Birth ....

....

Home Address(es) ....

....

....

....

Occupation ....

....

Religion ....

Date of Marriage(s) ....

....

Date of Death ....

Place of Burial ....

....

GREAT-GRANDMOTHER'S BROTHERS (GREAT-GREAT-UNCLES)

Surname ....

Given Name(s) ....

....

Nationality ....

Date of Birth ....

Place of Birth ....

....

Home Address(es) ....

....

....

....

Occupation ....

....

Religion ....

Date of Marriage(s) ....

....

Date of Death ....

Place of Burial ....

....

GREAT-GRANDMOTHER'S SISTERS (GREAT-GREAT-AUNTS)

Surname ....

Given Name(s) ....

....

Nationality ....

Date of Birth ....

Place of Birth ....

....

Home Address(es) ....

....

....

....

Occupation ....

....

Religion ....

Date of Marriage(s) ....

....

Married Name ....

Date of Death ....

Place of Burial ....

GREAT-GRANDMOTHER'S SISTERS (GREAT-GREAT-AUNTS)

Surname	....	....	....
Given Name(s)	....	....	....
	....	....	....
Nationality	....	....	....
Date of Birth	....	....	....
Place of Birth	....	....	....
	....	....	....
Home Address(es)	....	....	....
	....	....	....
	....	....	....
	....	....	....
Occupation	....	....	....
	....	....	....
Religion	....	....	....
Date of Marriage(s)	....	....	....
	....	....	....
Married Name	....	....	....
Date of Death	....	....	....
Place of Burial	....	....	....

ADDITIONAL INFORMATION

MATERNAL LINE

MOTHER

Surname ....   Additional Information

Given Name(s) ....

....

Nationality ....

Date of Birth ....

Place of Birth ....

....

Home Address(es) ....

....

....

....

Occupation ....

....

Religion ....

Date of Marriage(s) ....

....

Married Name ....

Date of Death ....

Place of Burial ....

MOTHER'S BROTHERS (UNCLES)

Surname ....

Given Name(s) ....

....

Nationality ....

Date of Birth ....

Place of Birth ....

....

Home Address(es) ....

....

....

....

Occupation ....

....

Religion ....

Date of Marriage(s) ....

....

Date of Death ....

Place of Burial ....

....

MOTHER'S BROTHERS (UNCLES)

Surname ....

Given Name(s) ....

....

Nationality ....

Date of Birth ....

Place of Birth ....

....

Home Address(es) ....

....

....

....

Occupation ....

....

Religion ....

Date of Marriage(s) ....

....

Date of Death ....

Place of Burial ....

....

MOTHER'S BROTHERS' CHILDREN (FIRST COUSINS)

Surname .... Child of ....

Given Name(s) .... and ....

Surname .... Child of ....

Given Name(s) .... and ....

Surname .... Child of ....

Given Name(s) .... and ....

Surname .... Child of ....

Given Name(s) .... and ....

Surname .... Child of ....

Given Name(s) .... and ....

Surname .... Child of ....

Given Name(s) .... and ....

Surname .... Child of ....

Given Name(s) .... and ....

Surname .... Child of ....

Given Name(s) .... and ....

Surname .... Child of ....

Given Name(s) .... and ....

MOTHER'S BROTHERS' CHILDREN (FIRST COUSINS)

Surname ....   Child of ....

Given Name(s) ....   and ....

Surname ....   Child of ....

Given Name(s) ....   and ....

Surname ....   Child of ....

Given Name(s) ....   and ....

Surname ....   Child of ....

Given Name(s) ....   and ....

Surname ....   Child of ....

Given Name(s) ....   and ....

Surname ....   Child of ....

Given Name(s) ....   and ....

Surname ....   Child of ....

Given Name(s) ....   and ....

Surname ....   Child of ....

Given Name(s) ....   and ....

Surname ....   Child of ....

Given Name(s) ....   and ....

MOTHER'S SISTERS (AUNTS)

Surname	....	....	....
Given Name(s)	....	....	....
	....	....	....
Nationality	....	....	....
Date of Birth	....	....	....
Place of Birth	....	....	....
	....	....	....
Home Address(es)	....	....	....
	....	....	....
	....	....	....
	....	....	....
Occupation	....	....	....
	....	....	....
Religion	....	....	....
Date of Marriage(s)	....	....	....
	....	....	....
Married Name	....	....	....
Date of Death	....	....	....
Place of Burial	....	....	....

MOTHER'S SISTERS (AUNTS)

Surname	....	....	....
Given Name(s)	....	....	....
	....	....	....
Nationality	....	....	....
Date of Birth	....	....	....
Place of Birth	....	....	....
	....	....	....
Home Address(es)	....	....	....
	....	....	....
	....	....	....
Occupation	....	....	....
	....	....	....
Religion	....	....	....
Date of Marriage(s)	....	....	....
	....	....	....
Married Name	....	....	....
Date of Death	....	....	....
Place of Burial	....	....	....

MOTHER'S SISTERS' CHILDREN (FIRST COUSINS)

Surname ....

Given Name(s) ....

Surname ....

Given Name(s) ....

Surname ....

Given Name(s) ....

Surname ....

Given Name(s) ....

Surname ....

Given Name(s) ....

Surname ....

Given Name(s) ....

Surname ....

Given Name(s) ....

Surname ....

Given Name(s) ....

Child of ....

and ....

Child of ....

and ....

Child of ....

and ....

Child of ....

and ....

Child of ....

and ....

Child of ....

and ....

Child of ....

and ....

Child of ....

and ....

MOTHER'S SISTERS' CHILDREN (FIRST COUSINS)

Surname .... Child of ....

Given Name(s) .... and ....

Surname .... Child of ....

Given Name(s) .... and ....

Surname .... Child of ....

Given Name(s) .... and ....

Surname .... Child of ....

Given Name(s) .... and ....

Surname .... Child of ....

Given Name(s) .... and ....

Surname .... Child of ....

Given Name(s) .... and ....

Surname .... Child of ....

Given Name(s) .... and ....

Surname .... Child of ....

Given Name(s) .... and ....

Surname .... Child of ....

Given Name(s) .... and ....

GRANDFATHER (MOTHER'S FATHER)

Surname .... Additional Information

Given Name(s) ....

....

Nationality ....

Date of Birth ....

Place of Birth ....

....

Home Address(es) ....

....

....

....

Occupation ....

....

Religion ....

Date of Marriage(s) ....

....

Date of Death ....

Place of Burial ....

....

GRANDFATHER'S BROTHERS (GREAT-UNCLES)

Surname	....	....	....
Given Name(s)	....	....	....
	....	....	....
Nationality	....	....	....
Date of Birth	....	....	....
Place of Birth	....	....	....
	....	....	....
Home Address(es)	....	....	....
	....	....	....
	....	....	....
	....	....	....
Occupation	....	....	....
	....	....	....
Religion	....	....	....
Date of Marriage(s)	....	....	....
	....	....	....
Date of Death	....	....	....
Place of Burial	....	....	....
	....	....	....

GRANDFATHER'S BROTHERS (GREAT-UNCLES)

Surname	....	....	....
Given Name(s)	....	....	....
	....	....	....
Nationality	....	....	....
Date of Birth	....	....	....
Place of Birth	....	....	....
	....	....	....
Home Address(es)	....	....	....
	....	....	....
	....	....	....
	....	....	....
Occupation	....	....	....
	....	....	....
Religion	....	....	....
Date of Marriage(s)	....	....	....
	....	....	....
Date of Death	....	....	....
Place of Burial	....	....	....
	....	....	....

GRANDFATHER'S BROTHERS' CHILDREN (FIRST COUSINS ONCE REMOVED)

Surname .... Child of ....

Given Name(s) .... and ....

Surname .... Child of ....

Given Name(s) .... and ....

Surname .... Child of ....

Given Name(s) .... and ....

Surname .... Child of ....

Given Name(s) .... and ....

Surname .... Child of ....

Given Name(s) .... and ....

Surname .... Child of ....

Given Name(s) .... and ....

Surname .... Child of ....

Given Name(s) .... and ....

Surname .... Child of ....

Given Name(s) .... and ....

GRANDFATHER'S SISTERS (GREAT-AUNTS)

Surname	....	....	....
Given Name(s)	....	....	....
	....	....	....
Nationality	....	....	....
Date of Birth	....	....	....
Place of Birth	....	....	....
	....	....	....
Home Address(es)	....	....	....
	....	....	....
	....	....	....
	....	....	....
Occupation	....	....	....
	....	....	....
Religion	....	....	....
Date of Marriage(s)	....	....	....
	....	....	....
Married Name	....	....	....
Date of Death	....	....	....
Place of Burial	....	....	....

GRANDFATHER'S SISTERS (GREAT-AUNTS)

Surname	....	....	....
Given Name(s)	....	....	....
	....	....	....
Nationality	....	....	....
Date of Birth	....	....	....
Place of Birth	....	....	....
	....	....	....
Home Address(es)	....	....	....
	....	....	....
	....	....	....
	....	....	....
Occupation	....	....	....
	....	....	....
Religion	....	....	....
Date of Marriage(s)	....	....	....
	....	....	....
Married Name	....	....	....
Date of Death	....	....	....
Place of Burial	....	....	....

GRANDFATHER'S SISTERS' CHILDREN (FIRST COUSINS ONCE REMOVED)

Surname	....	Child of	....
Given Name(s)	....	and	....
Surname	....	Child of	....
Given Name(s)	....	and	....
Surname	....	Child of	....
Given Name(s)	....	and	....
Surname	....	Child of	....
Given Name(s)	....	and	....
Surname	....	Child of	....
Given Name(s)	....	and	....
Surname	....	Child of	....
Given Name(s)	....	and	....
Surname	....	Child of	....
Given Name(s)	....	and	....
Surname	....	Child of	....
Given Name(s)	....	and	....
Surname	....	Child of	....
Given Name(s)	....	and	....

GRANDMOTHER (MOTHER'S MOTHER)

Surname .... Additional Information

Given Name(s) ....

....

Nationality ....

Date of Birth ....

Place of Birth ....

....

Home Address(es) ....

....

....

....

Occupation ....

....

Religion ....

Date of Marriage(s) ....

....

Married Name ....

Date of Death ....

Place of Burial ....

GRANDMOTHER'S BROTHERS (GREAT-UNCLES)

Surname ....

Given Name(s) ....

....

Nationality ....

Date of Birth ....

Place of Birth ....

....

Home Address(es) ....

....

....

....

Occupation ....

....

Religion ....

Date of Marriage(s) ....

....

Date of Death ....

Place of Burial ....

....

GRANDMOTHER'S BROTHERS (GREAT-UNCLES)

Surname	....	....	....
Given Name(s)	....	....	....
	....	....	....
Nationality	....	....	....
Date of Birth	....	....	....
Place of Birth	....	....	....
	....	....	....
Home Address(es)	....	....	....
	....	....	....
	....	....	....
	....	....	....
Occupation	....	....	....
	....	....	....
Religion	....	....	....
Date of Marriage(s)	....	....	....
	....	....	....
Date of Death	....	....	....
Place of Burial	....	....	....
	....	....	....

GRANDMOTHER'S BROTHERS' CHILDREN (FIRST COUSINS ONCE REMOVED)

Surname	Child of ....
Given Name(s)	and ....
Surname	Child of ....
Given Name(s)	and ....
Surname	Child of ....
Given Name(s)	and ....
Surname	Child of ....
Given Name(s)	and ....
Surname	Child of ....
Given Name(s)	and ....
Surname	Child of ....
Given Name(s)	and ....
Surname	Child of ....
Given Name(s)	and ....
Surname	Child of ....
Given Name(s)	and ....

GRANDMOTHER'S SISTERS (GREAT-AUNTS)

Surname			
Given Name(s)			
Nationality			
Date of Birth			
Place of Birth			
Home Address(es)			
Occupation			
Religion			
Date of Marriage(s)			
Married Name			
Date of Death			
Place of Burial			

GRANDMOTHER'S SISTERS (GREAT-AUNTS)

Surname	....	....	....
Given Name(s)	....	....	....
	....	....	....
Nationality	....	....	....
Date of Birth	....	....	....
Place of Birth	....	....	....
	....	....	....
Home Address(es)	....	....	....
	....	....	....
	....	....	....
	....	....	....
Occupation	....	....	....
	....	....	....
Religion	....	....	....
Date of Marriage(s)	....	....	....
	....	....	....
Married Name	....	....	....
Date of Death	....	....	....
Place of Burial	....	....	....

GRANDMOTHER'S SISTERS' CHILDREN (FIRST COUSINS ONCE REMOVED)

Surname	....	Child of	....
Given Name(s)	....	and	....
Surname	....	Child of	....
Given Name(s)	....	and	....
Surname	....	Child of	....
Given Name(s)	....	and	....
Surname	....	Child of	....
Given Name(s)	....	and	....
Surname	....	Child of	....
Given Name(s)	....	and	....
Surname	....	Child of	....
Given Name(s)	....	and	....
Surname	....	Child of	....
Given Name(s)	....	and	....
Surname	....	Child of	....
Given Name(s)	....	and	....

GREAT-GRANDFATHER (MOTHER'S FATHER'S FATHER)

Surname . . . .   Additional Information

Given Name(s) . . . .

. . . .

Nationality . . . .

Date of Birth . . . .

Place of Birth . . . .

. . . .

Home Address(es) . . . .

. . . .

. . . .

. . . .

Occupation . . . .

. . . .

Religion . . . .

Date of Marriage(s) . . . .

. . . .

Date of Death . . . .

Place of Burial . . . .

. . . .

GREAT-GRANDFATHER'S BROTHERS (GREAT-GREAT-UNCLES)

Surname ....

Given Name(s) ....

....

Nationality ....

Date of Birth ....

Place of Birth ....

....

Home Address(es) ....

....

....

....

Occupation ....

....

Religion ....

Date of Marriage(s) ....

....

Date of Death ....

Place of Burial ....

....

GREAT-GRANDFATHER'S BROTHERS (GREAT-GREAT-UNCLES)

Surname	. . . .	. . . .	. . . .
Given Name(s)	. . . .	. . . .	. . . .
	. . . .	. . . .	. . . .
Nationality	. . . .	. . . .	. . . .
Date of Birth	. . . .	. . . .	. . . .
Place of Birth	. . . .	. . . .	. . . .
	. . . .	. . . .	. . . .
Home Address(es)	. . . .	. . . .	. . . .
	. . . .	. . . .	. . . .
	. . . .	. . . .	. . . .
	. . . .	. . . .	. . . .
Occupation	. . . .	. . . .	. . . .
	. . . .	. . . .	. . . .
Religion	. . . .	. . . .	. . . .
Date of Marriage(s)	. . . .	. . . .	. . . .
	. . . .	. . . .	. . . .
Date of Death	. . . .	. . . .	. . . .
Place of Burial	. . . .	. . . .	. . . .
	. . . .	. . . .	. . . .

GREAT-GRANDFATHER'S SISTERS (GREAT-GREAT-AUNTS)

Surname			
Given Name(s)			
Nationality			
Date of Birth			
Place of Birth			
Home Address(es)			
Occupation			
Religion			
Date of Marriage(s)			
Married Name			
Date of Death			
Place of Burial			

MATERNAL LINE

GREAT-GRANDFATHER'S SISTERS (GREAT-GREAT-AUNTS)

Surname	....	....	....
Given Name(s)	....	....	....
	....	....	....
Nationality	....	....	....
Date of Birth	....	....	....
Place of Birth	....	....	....
	....	....	....
Home Address(es)	....	....	....
	....	....	....
	....	....	....
	....	....	....
Occupation	....	....	....
	....	....	....
Religion	....	....	....
Date of Marriage(s)	....	....	....
	....	....	....
Married Name	....	....	....
Date of Death	....	....	....
Place of Burial	....	....	....

MATERNAL LINE

GREAT-GRANDMOTHER (MOTHER'S FATHER'S MOTHER)

Surname .... Additional Information

Given Name(s) ....

....

Nationality ....

Date of Birth ....

Place of Birth ....

....

Home Address(es) ....

....

....

....

Occupation ....

....

Religion ....

Date of Marriage(s) ....

....

Married Name ....

Date of Death ....

Place of Burial ....

GREAT-GRANDMOTHER'S BROTHERS (GREAT-GREAT-UNCLES)

Surname	....	....	....
Given Name(s)	....	....	....
	....	....	....
Nationality	....	....	....
Date of Birth	....	....	....
Place of Birth	....	....	....
	....	....	....
Home Address(es)	....	....	....
	....	....	....
	....	....	....
	....	....	....
Occupation	....	....	....
	....	....	....
Religion	....	....	....
Date of Marriage(s)	....	....	....
	....	....	....
Date of Death	....	....	....
Place of Burial	....	....	....
	....	....	....

GREAT-GRANDMOTHER'S BROTHERS (GREAT-GREAT-UNCLES)

Surname ....

Given Name(s) ....

....

Nationality ....

Date of Birth ....

Place of Birth ....

....

Home Address(es) ....

....

....

....

Occupation ....

....

Religion ....

Date of Marriage(s) ....

....

Date of Death ....

Place of Burial ....

....

GREAT-GRANDMOTHER'S SISTERS (GREAT-GREAT-AUNTS)

Surname	....	....	....
Given Name(s)	....	....	....
	....	....	....
Nationality	....	....	....
Date of Birth	....	....	....
Place of Birth	....	....	....
	....	....	....
Home Address(es)	....	....	....
	....	....	....
	....	....	....
	....	....	....
Occupation	....	....	....
	....	....	....
Religion	....	....	....
Date of Marriage(s)	....	....	....
	....	....	....
Married Name	....	....	....
Date of Death	....	....	....
Place of Burial	....	....	....

GREAT-GRANDMOTHER'S SISTERS (GREAT-GREAT-AUNTS)

Surname	....	....	....
Given Name(s)	....	....	....
	....	....	....
Nationality	....	....	....
Date of Birth	....	....	....
Place of Birth	....	....	....
	....	....	....
Home Address(es)	....	....	....
	....	....	....
	....	....	....
	....	....	....
Occupation	....	....	....
	....	....	....
Religion	....	....	....
Date of Marriage(s)	....	....	....
	....	....	....
Married Name	....	....	....
Date of Death	....	....	....
Place of Burial	....	....	....

GREAT-GRANDFATHER (MOTHER'S MOTHER'S FATHER)

Surname ....   Additional Information

Given Name(s) ....

....

Nationality ....

Date of Birth ....

Place of Birth ....

....

Home Address(es) ....

....

....

....

Occupation ....

....

Religion ....

Date of Marriage(s) ....

....

Date of Death ....

Place of Burial ....

....

GREAT-GRANDFATHER'S BROTHERS (GREAT-GREAT-UNCLES)

Surname	....	....	....
Given Name(s)	....	....	....
	....	....	....
Nationality	....	....	....
Date of Birth	....	....	....
Place of Birth	....	....	....
	....	....	....
Home Address(es)	....	....	....
	....	....	....
	....	....	....
	....	....	....
Occupation	....	....	....
	....	....	....
Religion	....	....	....
Date of Marriage(s)	....	....	....
	....	....	....
Date of Death	....	....	....
Place of Burial	....	....	....
	....	....	....

GREAT-GRANDFATHER'S BROTHERS (GREAT-GREAT-UNCLES)

Surname	....	....	....
Given Name(s)	....	....	....
	....	....	....
Nationality	....	....	....
Date of Birth	....	....	....
Place of Birth	....	....	....
	....	....	....
Home Address(es)	....	....	....
	....	....	....
	....	....	....
	....	....	....
Occupation	....	....	....
	....	....	....
Religion	....	....	....
Date of Marriage(s)	....	....	....
	....	....	....
Date of Death	....	....	....
Place of Burial	....	....	....
	....	....	....

GREAT-GRANDFATHER'S SISTERS (GREAT-GREAT-AUNTS)

Surname	....	....	....
Given Name(s)	....	....	....
	....	....	....
Nationality	....	....	....
Date of Birth	....	....	....
Place of Birth	....	....	....
	....	....	....
Home Address(es)	....	....	....
	....	....	....
	....	....	....
	....	....	....
Occupation	....	....	....
	....	....	....
Religion	....	....	....
Date of Marriage(s)	....	....	....
	....	....	....
Married Name	....	....	....
Date of Death	....	....	....
Place of Burial	....	....	....

GREAT-GRANDFATHER'S SISTERS (GREAT-GREAT-AUNTS)

Surname ....

Given Name(s) ....

....

Nationality ....

Date of Birth ....

Place of Birth ....

....

Home Address(es) ....

....

....

....

Occupation ....

....

Religion ....

Date of Marriage(s) ....

....

Married Name ....

Date of Death ....

Place of Burial ....

GREAT-GRANDMOTHER (MOTHER'S MOTHER'S MOTHER)

Surname . . . .   Additional Information

Given Name(s) . . . .

. . . .

Nationality . . . .

Date of Birth . . . .

Place of Birth . . . .

. . . .

Home Address(es) . . . .

. . . .

. . . .

. . . .

Occupation . . . .

. . . .

Religion . . . .

Date of Marriage(s) . . . .

. . . .

Married Name . . . .

Date of Death . . . .

Place of Burial . . . .

GREAT-GRANDMOTHER'S BROTHER (GREAT-GREAT-UNCLES)

Surname			
Given Name(s)			
Nationality			
Date of Birth			
Place of Birth			
Home Address(es)			
Occupation			
Religion			
Date of Marriage(s)			
Date of Death			
Place of Burial			

GREAT-GRANDMOTHER'S BROTHERS (GREAT-GREAT-UNCLES)

Surname	....	....	....
Given Name(s)	....	....	....
	....	....	....
Nationality	....	....	....
Date of Birth	....	....	....
Place of Birth	....	....	....
	....	....	....
Home Address(es)	....	....	....
	....	....	....
	....	....	....
	....	....	....
Occupation	....	....	....
	....	....	....
Religion	....	....	....
Date of Marriage(s)	....	....	....
	....	....	....
Date of Death	....	....	....
Place of Burial	....	....	....
	....	....	....

GREAT-GRANDMOTHER'S SISTERS (GREAT-GREAT-AUNTS)

Surname	....	....	....
Given Name(s)	....	....	....
	....	....	....
Nationality	....	....	....
Date of Birth	....	....	....
Place of Birth	....	....	....
	....	....	....
Home Address(es)	....	....	....
	....	....	....
	....	....	....
	....	....	....
Occupation	....	....	....
	....	....	....
Religion	....	....	....
Date of Marriage(s)	....	....	....
	....	....	....
Married Name	....	....	....
Date of Death	....	....	....
Place of Burial	....	....	....

MATERNAL LINE

GREAT-GRANDMOTHER'S SISTERS (GREAT-GREAT-AUNTS)

Surname	....	....	....
Given Name(s)	....	....	....
	....	....	....
Nationality	....	....	....
Date of Birth	....	....	....
Place of Birth	....	....	....
	....	....	....
Home Address(es)	....	....	....
	....	....	....
	....	....	....
	....	....	....
Occupation	....	....	....
	....	....	....
Religion	....	....	....
Date of Marriage(s)	....	....	....
	....	....	....
Married Name	....	....	....
Date of Death	....	....	....
Place of Burial	....	....	....

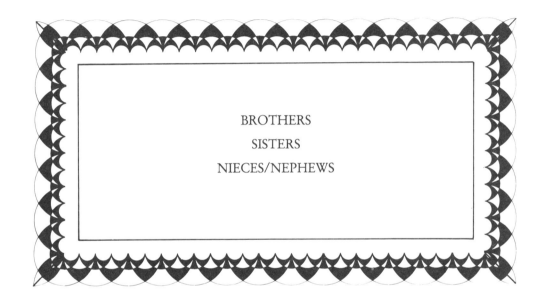

BROTHERS

SISTERS

NIECES/NEPHEWS

BROTHERS

Surname ....

Given Name(s) ....

....

Nationality ....

Date of Birth ....

Place of Birth ....

....

Home Address(es) ....

....

....

....

Occupation ....

....

Religion ....

Date of Marriage(s) ....

....

Additional Information ....

....

....

IMMEDIATE FAMILY

BROTHERS

Surname ....

Given Name(s) ....

....

Nationality ....

Date of Birth ....

Place of Birth ....

....

Home Address(es) ....

....

....

....

Occupation ....

....

Religion ....

Date of Marriage(s) ....

....

Additional Information ....

....

....

IMMEDIATE FAMILY

BROTHERS' CHILDREN (NIECES/NEPHEWS)

Surname	....	Child of	....
Given Name(s)	....	and	....
Surname	....	Child of	....
Given Name(s)	....	and	....
Surname	....	Child of	....
Given Name(s)	....	and	....
Surname	....	Child of	....
Given Name(s)	....	and	....
Surname	....	Child of	....
Given Name(s)	....	and	....
Surname	....	Child of	....
Given Name(s)	....	and	....
Surname	....	Child of	....
Given Name(s)	....	and	....
Surname	....	Child of	....
Given Name(s)	....	and	....

IMMEDIATE FAMILY

BROTHERS' CHILDREN (NIECES/NEPHEWS)

Surname ....

Given Name(s) ....

Surname ....

Given Name(s) ....

Surname ....

Given Name(s) ....

Surname ....

Given Name(s) ....

Surname ....

Given Name(s) ....

Surname ....

Given Name(s) ....

Surname ....

Given Name(s) ....

Surname ....

Given Name(s) ....

Child of ....

and ....

Child of ....

and ....

Child of ....

and ....

Child of ....

and ....

Child of ....

and ....

Child of ....

and ....

Child of ....

and ....

Child of ....

and ....

SISTERS

Surname ....

Given Name(s) ....

....

Nationality ....

Date of Birth ....

Place of Birth ....

....

Home Address(es) ....

....

....

Occupation ....

....

Religion ....

Date of Marriage(s) ....

....

Married Name ....

Additional Information ....

....

....

SISTERS

Surname	....	....	....
Given Name(s)	....	....	....
	....	....	....
Nationality	....	....	....
Date of Birth	....	....	....
Place of Birth	....	....	....
	....	....	....
Home Address(es)	....	....	....
	....	....	....
	....	....	....
Occupation	....	....	....
	....	....	....
Religion	....	....	....
Date of Marriage(s)	....	....	....
	....	....	....
Married Name	....	....	....
Additional Information	....	....	....
	....	....	....
	....	....	....

IMMEDIATE FAMILY

SISTERS' CHILDREN (NIECES/NEPHEWS)

Surname .... Child of ....

Given Name(s) .... and ....

Surname .... Child of ....

Given Name(s) .... and ....

Surname .... Child of ....

Given Name(s) .... and ....

Surname .... Child of ....

Given Name(s) .... and ....

Surname .... Child of ....

Given Name(s) .... and ....

Surname .... Child of ....

Given Name(s) .... and ....

Surname .... Child of ....

Given Name(s) .... and ....

Surname .... Child of ....

Given Name(s) .... and ....

Surname .... Child of ....

Given Name(s) .... and ....

SISTERS' CHILDREN (NIECES/NEPHEWS)

Surname . . . .   Child of . . . .

Given Name(s) . . . .   and . . . .

Surname . . . .   Child of . . . .

Given Name(s) . . . .   and . . . .

Surname . . . .   Child of . . . .

Given Name(s) . . . .   and . . . .

Surname . . . .   Child of . . . .

Given Name(s) . . . .   and . . . .

Surname . . . .   Child of . . . .

Given Name(s) . . . .   and . . . .

Surname . . . .   Child of . . . .

Given Name(s) . . . .   and . . . .

Surname . . . .   Child of . . . .

Given Name(s) . . . .   and . . . .

Surname . . . .   Child of . . . .

Given Name(s) . . . .   and . . . .

BROTHERS

Surname	....	....	....
Given Name(s)	....	....	....
	....	....	....
Nationality	....	....	....
Date of Birth	....	....	....
Place of Birth	....	....	....
	....	....	....
Home Address(es)	....	....	....
	....	....	....
	....	....	....
	....	....	....
Occupation	....	....	....
	....	....	....
Religion	....	....	....
Date of Marriage(s)	....	....	....
	....	....	....
Additional Information	....	....	....
	....	....	....
	....	....	....

BROTHERS

Surname ....

Given Name(s) ....

....

Nationality ....

Date of Birth ....

Place of Birth ....

....

Home Address(es) ....

....

....

....

Occupation ....

....

Religion ....

Date of Marriage(s) ....

....

Additional Information ....

....

....

BROTHERS' CHILDREN (NIECES/NEPHEWS)

Surname	Child of	
Given Name(s)	and	
Surname	Child of	
Given Name(s)	and	
Surname	Child of	
Given Name(s)	and	
Surname	Child of	
Given Name(s)	and	
Surname	Child of	
Given Name(s)	and	
Surname	Child of	
Given Name(s)	and	
Surname	Child of	
Given Name(s)	and	
Surname	Child of	
Given Name(s)	and	

BROTHERS' CHILDREN (NIECES/NEPHEWS)

Surname . . . .

Given Name(s) . . . .

Surname . . . .

Given Name(s) . . . .

Surname . . . .

Given Name(s) . . . .

Surname . . . .

Given Name(s) . . . .

Surname . . . .

Given Name(s) . . . .

Surname . . . .

Given Name(s) . . . .

Surname . . . .

Given Name(s) . . . .

Surname . . . .

Given Name(s) . . . .

Child of . . . .

and . . . .

Child of . . . .

and . . . .

Child of . . . .

and . . . .

Child of . . . .

and . . . .

Child of . . . .

and . . . .

Child of . . . .

and . . . .

Child of . . . .

and . . . .

Child of . . . .

and . . . .

SISTERS

Surname	....	....	....
Given Name(s)	....	....	....
	....	....	....
Nationality	....	....	....
Date of Birth	....	....	....
Place of Birth	....	....	....
	....	....	....
Home Address(es)	....	....	....
	....	....	....
	....	....	....
Occupation	....	....	....
	....	....	....
Religion	....	....	....
Date of Marriage(s)	....	....	....
	....	....	....
Married Name	....	....	....
Additional Information	....	....	....
	....	....	....
	....	....	....

SISTERS

Surname ....

Given Name(s) ....

....

Nationality ....

Date of Birth ....

Place of Birth ....

....

Home Address(es) ....

....

....

Occupation ....

....

Religion ....

Date of Marriage(s) ....

....

Married Name ....

Additional Information ....

....

....

SISTERS' CHILDREN (NIECES/NEPHEWS)

Surname . . . . Child of . . . .

Given Name(s) . . . . and . . . .

Surname . . . . Child of . . . .

Given Name(s) . . . . and . . . .

Surname . . . . Child of . . . .

Given Name(s) . . . . and . . . .

Surname . . . . Child of . . . .

Given Name(s) . . . . and . . . .

Surname . . . . Child of . . . .

Given Name(s) . . . . and . . . .

Surname . . . . Child of . . . .

Given Name(s) . . . . and . . . .

Surname . . . . Child of . . . .

Given Name(s) . . . . and . . . .

Surname . . . . Child of . . . .

Given Name(s) . . . . and . . . .

SISTERS' CHILDREN (NIECES/NEPHEWS)

Surname	....	Child of	....
Given Name(s)	....	and	....
Surname	....	Child of	....
Given Name(s)	....	and	....
Surname	....	Child of	....
Given Name(s)	....	and	....
Surname	....	Child of	....
Given Name(s)	....	and	....
Surname	....	Child of	....
Given Name(s)	....	and	....
Surname	....	Child of	....
Given Name(s)	....	and	....
Surname	....	Child of	....
Given Name(s)	....	and	....
Surname	....	Child of	....
Given Name(s)	....	and	....
Surname	....	Child of	....
Given Name(s)	....	and	....

ADDITIONAL INFORMATION

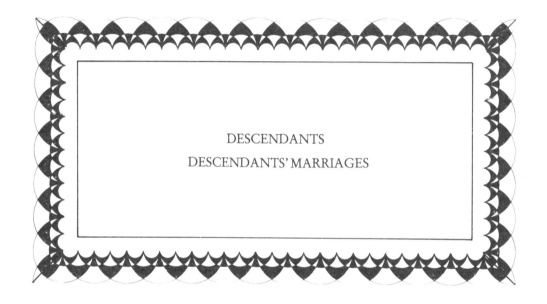

DESCENDANTS

DESCENDANTS' MARRIAGES

DESCENDANTS

SONS

Name(s)	. . . .	. . . .	. . . .
	. . . .	. . . .	. . . .
Date of Birth	. . . .	. . . .	. . . .
Place of Birth	. . . .	. . . .	. . . .
	. . . .	. . . .	. . . .
Religion	. . . .	. . . .	. . . .
Ceremony held in	. . . .	. . . .	. . . .
	. . . .	. . . .	. . . .
Date of Ceremony	. . . .	. . . .	. . . .
Officiator	. . . .	. . . .	. . . .
Godfather	. . . .	. . . .	. . . .
Godmother	. . . .	. . . .	. . . .
Additional Information	. . . .	. . . .	. . . .
	. . . .	. . . .	. . . .
	. . . .	. . . .	. . . .
	. . . .	. . . .	. . . .
	. . . .	. . . .	. . . .

DESCENDANTS

SONS

Name(s) ....

....

Date of Birth ....

Place of Birth ....

....

Religion ....

Ceremony held in ....

....

Date of Ceremony ....

Officiator ....

Godfather ....

Godmother ....

Additional Information ....

....

....

....

....

....

DAUGHTERS

Name(s) ....

....

Date of Birth ....

Place of Birth ....

....

Religion ....

Ceremony held in ....

....

Date of Ceremony ....

Officiator ....

Godfather ....

Godmother ....

Additional Information ....

....

....

....

....

....

DESCENDANTS

DAUGHTERS

Name(s) ....

....

Date of Birth ....

Place of Birth ....

....

Religion ....

Ceremony held in ....

....

Date of Ceremony ....

Officiator ....

Godfather ....

Godmother ....

Additional Information ....

....

....

....

....

....

SONS

Name(s) ....
....

Date ....

to ....

....

Daughter of ....

of ....

....

....

Place of Marriage ....

Officiator ....

Bestman ....

Bridesmaid(s) ....

....

....

....

Additional Information ....

....

....

MARRIAGES OF DESCENDANTS

SONS

Name(s) ....

....

Date ....

to ....

....

Daughter of ....

of ....

....

....

Place of Marriage ....

Officiator ....

Bestman ....

Bridesmaid(s) ....

....

....

....

Additional Information ....

....

....

DAUGHTERS

Name(s) ....

....

Date ....

to ....

....

Son of ....

of ....

....

....

Place of Marriage ....

Officiator ....

Bestman ....

Bridesmaid(s) ....

....

....

....

Additional Information ....

....

....

MARRIAGES OF DESCENDANTS

DAUGHTERS

Name(s) ....

....

Date ....

to ....

....

Son of ....

of ....

....

....

Place of Marriage ....

Officiator ....

Bestman ....

Bridesmaid(s) ....

....

....

....

Additional Information ....

....

....

GRANDCHILDREN

MALE

Surname	....	....	....
Given Name(s)	....	....	....
	....	....	....
Date of Birth	....	....	....
Parents	....	....	....
	....	....	....
Religion	....	....	....
Ceremony held in	....	....	....
	....	....	....
Officiator	....	....	....
Godfather	....	....	....
Godmother	....	....	....
Additional Information	....	....	....
	....	....	....
	....	....	....
	....	....	....
	....	....	....
	....	....	....

GRANDCHILDREN

MALE

Surname			
Given Name(s)			
Date of Birth			
Parents			
Religion			
Ceremony held in			
Officiator			
Godfather			
Godmother			
Additional Information			

FEMALE

Surname	....	....	....
Given Name(s)	....	....	....
	....	....	....
Date of Birth	....	....	....
Parents	....	....	....
	....	....	....
Religion	....	....	....
Ceremony held in	....	....	....
	....	....	....
Officiator	....	....	....
Godfather	....	....	....
Godmother	....	....	....
Additional Information	....	....	....
	....	....	....
	....	....	....
	....	....	....
	....	....	....
	....	....	....

GRANDCHILDREN

FEMALE

Surname	....	....	....
Given Name(s)	....	....	....
	....	....	....
Date of Birth	....	....	....
Parents	....	....	....
	....	....	....
Religion	....	....	....
Ceremony held in	....	....	....
	....	....	....
Officiator	....	....	....
Godfather	....	....	....
Godmother	....	....	....
Additional Information	....	....	....
	....	....	....
	....	....	....
	....	....	....
	....	....	....
	....	....	....

GREAT-GRANDCHILDREN

Name(s)   Date of Birth   Parents

. . . .

. . . .

. . . .

. . . .

. . . .

. . . .

. . . .

. . . .

. . . .

. . . .

. . . .

. . . .

. . . .

. . . .

. . . .

. . . .

. . . .

GREAT-GRANDCHILDREN

Name(s)	Date of Birth	Parents
....	....	....
....	....	....
....	....	....
....	....	....
....	....	....
....	....	....
....	....	....
....	....	....
....	....	....
....	....	....
....	....	....
....	....	....
....	....	....
....	....	....
....	....	....
....	....	....

....
....
....
....
....
....
....
....
....
....
....
....
....
....
....
....

ADDITIONAL INFORMATION

BIRTHS

Date	Name	Address

BIRTHS

Date	Name	Address

250

MARRIAGES

Date	Names	Address
. . . .	. . . .	. . . .
. . . .	. . . .	. . . .
. . . .	. . . .	. . . .
. . . .	. . . .	. . . .
. . . .	. . . .	. . . .
. . . .	. . . .	. . . .
. . . .	. . . .	. . . .
. . . .	. . . .	. . . .
. . . .	. . . .	. . . .
. . . .	. . . .	. . . .
. . . .	. . . .	. . . .
. . . .	. . . .	. . . .
. . . .	. . . .	. . . .
. . . .	. . . .	. . . .
. . . .	. . . .	. . . .

MARRIAGES

Date	Names	Address

DEATHS

Date	Name	Place of Burial

DEATHS

Date	Name	Place of Burial
. . . .	. . . .	. . . .
. . . .	. . . .	. . . .
. . . .	. . . .	. . . .
. . . .	. . . .	. . . .
. . . .	. . . .	. . . .
. . . .	. . . .	. . . .
. . . .	. . . .	. . . .
. . . .	. . . .	. . . .
. . . .	. . . .	. . . .
. . . .	. . . .	. . . .
. . . .	. . . .	. . . .
. . . .	. . . .	. . . .
. . . .	. . . .	. . . .
. . . .	. . . .	. . . .
. . . .	. . . .	. . . .

ADDITIONAL INFORMATION